MARTIN LUTHER
KING, JR.

other titles in the **BIOGRAPHY**® *book series:*

Muhammad Ali

Al Capone

Katharine Hepburn

Mickey Mantle

Jacqueline Kennedy Onassis

Pope John Paul II

Ronald Reagan

MARTIN LUTHER KING, JR.

V. P. Franklin

A Balliett & Fitzgerald Book

PARK LANE

NEW YORK

This 1998 edition is published by Park Lane Press,
a division of Random House Value Publishing, Inc.,
a Random House Company
201 East 50th Street, New York, New York 10022

A&E's acclaimed BIOGRAPHY series is available on videocassette from
A&E Home Video. Call 1-800-423-1212 to order.

A&E and **BIOGRAPHY** are trademarks of A&E Television Networks,
registered in the United States and other countries.

Park Lane Press and colophon are trademarks of
Random House Value Publishing, Inc.

Random House, Inc.
New York • Toronto • London • Sydney • Auckland
www.randomhouse.com

Printed and bound in the United States of America

A Balliett & Fitzgerald Book
Series Editor: Thomas Dyja
Book Design: Lisa Govan, Susan Canavan
Production Editors: Maria Fernandez, Mike Walters
Photo Research: Maria Fernandez
Assistant Editor: Irene Agriodimas

Library of Congress Cataloging-in-Publication Data

Franklin, V. P. (Vincent P.), 1947–
    Martin Luther King, Jr. / V. P. Franklin.   —1st ed.
            p.   cm.   —(Biography)
    "A Balliett & Fitzgerald book."
        Includes bibliographical (p. 172) references and index.
            1. King, Martin Luther, Jr., 1929–1968. 2. Afro-Americans—
Biography. 3. Civil rights workers—United States—Biography.
4. Baptists—United States—Clergy—Biography. 5. Afro-Americans—
Civil Rights—History—20th century.
I. Title.   II. Series: Biography (Park Lane Press)
E185.97.K5F75   1998
323'.092.—dc21
(B)   98-22898
                                                          CIP

ISBN 0-517-20098-8
10 9 8 7 6 5 4 3 2 1
First Edition

CONTENTS

1. THIS LITTLE LIGHT OF MINE   3

2. WHAT SHALL I DO?   19

3. OH, WASN'T THAT A DAY   35

4. THERE IS A BALM IN GILEAD   65

5. GOD LAID HIS HANDS ON ME   95

6. WE SHALL OVERCOME   117

7. SEE WHAT THE END WILL BE   139

chronology   169

bibliography   172

sources   175

index   181

acknowledgments   185

Martin Luther King, Jr., front, right

CHAPTER ONE

THIS LITTLE LIGHT OF MINE

James King and his wife, Delia Lindsey King, could never agree on what to name their oldest son. The couple had been married in Stockbridge, Georgia, on August 20, 1895, and their first daughter, Woodie Clara, was born the following year. Their first son was born on December 19, 1897, and Delia King decided to name him Michael, after the archangel in the Old Testament; but her husband James King really had hoped to name the child after two of his brothers, Martin and Luther. While his mother always called her oldest son Michael, everyone else called him Mike, and his father never bothered to object.

James and Delia King had a total of ten children, nine of whom survived into adulthood to help their parents raise cotton and other crops on the land they worked as sharecroppers for Old Man Graves, the white landowner. When he was young,

Mike King never liked farming, but he always enjoyed going to Baptist church services with his mother. Martin Luther King, Sr., later known as "Daddy King," recalled that these early experiences provided the basis for his later decision to enter the ministry. "That call didn't come all at once, in any single place or at any one time. It built as an ever-deepening experience that I could not deny, even though I was so young, so unprepared to understand all of this."

Mike King became more immersed in the church and finally convinced the deacons at Floyd Chapel Baptist Church to grant him a license to preach. As a young preacher, Mike King became a Country Circuit minister or "C.C. Rider" who received food or live animals, rather than cash, in payment for conducting religious services. While young Reverend King learned a great deal from his experience as a rural minister, he still hated living and working on the farm. When he was nineteen, he left and joined his older sister Woodie Clara who had moved to Atlanta. While Mike had little difficulty getting menial jobs, it became very clear that his lack of education would greatly limit his career in the ministry. Having attended the one-room schoolhouse in Stockbridge, he decided to enroll at the Bryant School, a private institution, where to his chagrin he was placed in the fifth grade; he had difficulty keeping up with the coursework even at that level.

Young Reverend King remained at the Bryant School for five years, and during that period developed a crush on Alberta Christine Williams, the only daughter of Jennie Celeste Williams and Rev. Adam Daniel (A.D.) Williams, the pastor of Ebenezer Baptist Church, one of the most important black congregations in Atlanta. Mike had met Alberta when she was a sixteen-year-old student at Spelman Seminary through his sister Woodie Clara, a boarder in the Williams home. From the beginning, Mike King knew he wanted to marry Alberta, but he recognized that he would have to offer her more than his love to gain the blessing of her family. When the young couple began courting in 1920, Rev. A. D. Williams made it clear that his daughter's education was not going to be interrupted by marriage, and that for a preacher to be successful in the dynamic urban center that Atlanta was becoming, he would have to have a good education. The young preacher vowed to prepare himself for the future.

Rev. A. D. Williams had attended Morehouse College for one year, and he and Alberta urged Rev. King to enroll in some courses after King finished at the Bryant School. Because of his poor test results, King had to receive special permission from Morehouse president John Hope, but Rev. Mike King finally enrolled at Morehouse School of Religion in September 1926. As expected, he had great difficulty with his courses, many of which he failed and had to take over until he got a passing grade. But once King was enrolled at Morehouse, Rev. A. D. Williams gave his blessing to the marriage with Alberta. The wedding took place at Ebenezer Baptist Church on November 26, 1926. Rev. King's mother, Delia King, had died in 1924, but his father James and most of his brothers and sisters and friends from Atlanta attended the ceremony.

At this time Rev. King was pastoring two small churches, in the College Park and East Point sections of Atlanta. When he married Rev. A. D. Williams's daughter, most of the church members assumed young Rev. King would join his father-in-law in the pulpit at Ebenezer. And although the young couple moved into the Williams home, King maintained his strong commitment to the two small churches he pastored, continued his studies at Morehouse College, getting a B.A. in theology in June 1930, and resisted the pressures to have him join Ebenezer.

Alberta and Mike King's first child, Willie Christine, was born on September 11, 1927. Their second child, Michael Luther King, Jr., called "M.L.," was also born at his grandparents' home on Auburn Avenue after a difficult labor on January 15, 1929. Their third child, Alfred Daniel Williams King, ("A.D."), was born at home on March 21, 1930.

In the spring of 1931, Rev. A. D. Williams suffered a fatal heart attack. Through faith, determination, and willpower Williams had built Ebenezer Baptist Church into one of the most important religious institutions in black Atlanta, and hundreds of people, black and white, attended his funeral. With the death of his father-in-law, Rev. Mike King could no longer resist the call to the pulpit at Ebenezer.

The Great Depression had a devastating effect on the social and economic conditions of most Americans, but African Americans suffered more than others. In good times black workers were the "last hired, first fired," but with the economic downturn white workers were more than willing to take traditional Negro jobs at the lowest paying wages—"Negro wages." Even before the young pastor could attempt to assist his working-class members, Rev. King had to place the church itself on a sound economic footing. After city marshals padlocked the church's door in December 1931, Rev. King renegotiated the terms of the mortgage and was able to pay off the outstanding balance of $1,100 almost two years ahead of schedule. Ebenezer Baptist grew during the depression because Rev. Mike King preached and practiced the social gospel, which taught that the church must be involved in the daily lives of its members and the community in which it was located.

Ebenezer Baptist under Rev. Mike King fed the hungry, clothed the naked, and provided a range of social services for those in need. Rev. King's initial success in expanding the

THE SOCIAL GOSPEL MOVEMENT

The social wreckage that was created in many American cities with the rise of the industrial nation led to a widespread social reform movement at the end of the nineteenth century headed by upper-middle-class professionals and wealthy philanthropists. Whereas secular groups fought for improvements in urban public education and opened settlement houses in working-class and immigrant neighborhoods, Protestant reformers used the churches and religious institutions to provide social welfare services to the urban poor. Congregational minister Washington Gladden was critical of industrial capitalism and particularly interested in making organized religion more relevant to the lives of industrial workers. Gladden believed the sharp decline in churchgoing in many cities was due to the failure of the religious leaders to address the needs of the urban working class. Gladden, along with Walter Rauschenbusch, Dwight Moody, and other ministers who preached the new "social gospel," called upon urban churches to provide a wide array of social programs, not merely for the members of their congregations, but for all the residents in the neighborhood. While some Protestant denominations supported these calls for a new social emphasis in Christian churches, others did not; social gospelers were sometimes forced to abandon their denominational affiliations and to establish independent "institutional churches."

African-American ministers and congregations also were a part of this social gospel movement. In New York City, Chicago, Philadelphia, San Francisco, and other cities where black migrants arrived during the Great Migration, as well as the larger southern cities, institutional churches were opened by black Baptist and Methodist ministers, often with the assistance of progressive white reformers. Of particular importance to the poor black migrants was the availability of health care services in these churches. At the same time, campaigns for social justice and political advancement in these cities often traced their origins to these socially active congregations and ministers who took seriously their commitments to apply the Christian doctrine to the problems of modern society.

membership was overshadowed somewhat by the death of his father, James Albert King, in November 1933. Toward the end of his life, James King had moved into a house purchased by his children living in Atlanta, stopped drinking, and returned to the church. On his deathbed, he made one request of his oldest son—that Mike change his name to "Martin Luther" King, the name he had tried to give him at birth. Rev. King recalled that shortly after his father died, "I took the necessary legal papers and was therefore called Martin Luther King, Sr. And little Mike became M.L. to his family, although his friends were still calling him Mike many years later."

⚜ ⚜ ⚜

"Something greater than myself. . ."

Martin Luther King, Jr., began his schooling in the fall of 1933 at the Yonge Street Elementary School, at the same time as his sister Christine. However, in January 1934 his teacher overheard M.L. discussing his fifth birthday party, and, realizing he was underage, expelled the child. M.L. reentered the first grade in January 1935, but because he was far ahead of the other children, when he returned to school after summer vacation in 1935, he was placed in the second grade. In September 1936, he transferred to the David Howard Colored Elementary School, and remained there until he graduated from the sixth grade in June 1940. Young Martin Luther King, Jr., enrolled in the seventh grade at the Atlanta University Laboratory School, an experimental program associated with the School of Education. However, after only six months in the

Daddy King in 1983, with his daughter, Christine Farris.

eighth grade, he was placed in the ninth grade in January 1942, and in the fall of that year entered the tenth grade at Booker T. Washington High School.

M.L. enjoyed school, made many friends, and was a very good student. While school was important, M.L.'s home life was dominated by the church, with religious music of particular significance. Alberta King was the church organist and choir director, and Daddy King believed that "religious ideas and ideals are shaped as much by gospel songs as by gospel sermons." Young M.L. developed a beautiful singing voice and he often performed with his mother at religious gatherings and musical recitals. His favorite song was "I Want to Be More and More Like Jesus."

In his early years young Martin was very devoted to his grandmother, Jennie Celeste Williams. When she died of a heart attack on May 18, 1941, it triggered what his parents considered was M.L.'s second suicide attempt.

The first attempt took place once while M.L. and A.D. were playing around the house. A.D. was sliding down the bannister and ran right into their grandmother, Jennie Williams, knocking her unconscious. M.L. thought that she was dead. He became distraught, went to the second-floor window and jumped out. Fortunately, he was not seriously injured by the twelve-foot fall. On May 18, 1941, M.L. made his second attempt on his life. While speaking at a Woman's Day program at Mt. Olive Baptist Church, Jennie Williams suffered a fatal heart attack. That day M.L. had sneaked away from his house to go and watch a parade, and someone who saw him there told him what had happened. M.L. believed he was somehow to blame for his grandmother's death; he jumped out of the second-floor window, but again was not seriously injured.

Throughout his childhood Martin Luther King, Jr., was indirectly schooled in the art of political negotiation through the civil rights activities of his father. While Rev. King was able to surmount the myriad hurdles placed in the path of those black Atlantans who wanted to vote, most could not. In 1935, Rev. King wanted the black ministers of Atlanta to organize a rally and march on City Hall for voting rights. At the rally at

Ebenezer Baptist Church, Rev. King reminded those assembled that they needed to find a new way to deal with their problems. "I ain't gonna plow no more mules. I'll never step off the road again to let white folks pass. I am going to move forward to freedom." Several hundred marched through the streets to City Hall, and many were registered to vote. But that was merely a first step on the long road to political freedom.

Legal segregation, lack of voting and other civil rights, and economic exploitation were only the more obvious oppressions African Americans faced throughout the South and most of the country in the 1930s. The more subtle affronts and insults tended to gnaw away at the oppressed victim's self-concept and personal identity. Martin Luther King, Jr., wrote about his first encounter with the "race problem" in the United States, which most white Americans referred to inaccurately as the "Negro problem." Between the ages of three and six, one of M.L.'s closest friends was the son of the white man who owned the grocery store across the street from where he lived. The two boys played together almost every day, until they entered separate schools. After this, the friendship began to break off. "The climax came when he told me one day that his father had demanded that he would play with me no more. I will never forget what a shock that was for me."

When M.L. told his parents about what happened, "my mother took me on her lap and began telling me about slavery and how it ended with the Civil War. She tried to explain the divided system of the South . . . as a social condition rather than a natural order." Although his parents told him that he should not hate white people for the way they treated black people, "I did not conquer this anti-white feeling until I entered college and came into contact with white students through working in interracial organizations."

Martin Luther King, Jr., was very popular in high school, especially with the young ladies. With his deep baritone voice, refined behavior, and natty clothes (he gained the nickname "Tweed" because of the stylish suits he always wore), King had no trouble finding companions for school dances and the high-toned parties thrown by Atlanta's black elite. But he was also a good student. In his junior year King won the right to represent Booker T. Washington High School in Valdosta, Georgia, at the statewide Elks oratorical contest. M. L. King won second place with his speech on "The Negro and the Constitution," which was subsequently published in the 1944 edition of his high school yearbook. This momentous affair was marred, however, by an ugly racial insult on the return trip. When M.L. and his fellow students got on the bus, they sat in the first seats available. When white passengers began to enter, the bus driver ordered them to move to the rear, and at first they refused. The driver began to curse at them and threatened to call the police. Finally, their teacher, Sarah Grace Bradley, told them to get up and give the seats to the whites. M.L. was upset about the incident for quite some time. "It was a night I'll never forget. I don't think I have ever been so deeply angry in my life."

At the end of his junior year, M.L. was one of the promising high school juniors allowed to take a special admission test to Morehouse College. He was offered admission to Morehouse in September 1944. Enrollment at Morehouse had fallen off during the war years, and the college's president, Benjamin Mays, saw admitting promising high school juniors as a way of expanding the freshman class. Over the summer of 1944, and each of the next two summers, M.L. traveled with a group of Morehouse students to Simbury, Connecticut, to work on a tobacco farm. Although the work was extremely hard, he

Martin Luther King, Jr. (front row, third from left) during his years at Morehouse College.

enjoyed it and being on his own in the North. His letters home to his parents that summer revealed that he was disturbed by the racial discrimination in restaurants, waiting rooms, and other public accommodations in the South. "It was hard to understand why I could ride wherever I pleased on the train from New York to Washington, and then had to change to a Jim Crow car at the nation's capitol in order to continue the trip to Atlanta."

The Morehouse years had a great influence on shaping the mind and spirit of Martin Luther King, Jr. Although he was much younger than most of his classmates, Martin developed close relationships and made several lifelong friends. Though he majored in sociology, but did not excel academically in any of his courses except religion. Martin's favorite professor was George D. Kelsey, who was the director of the Department of

Religion. When he entered college, M.L. had no intention of going into the ministry, but he was favorably impressed by George Kelsey and Benjamin Mays, both of whom were ordained ministers. And there was the influence of his father, who "set forth a noble example I didn't [mind] following." Ultimately, the decision to enter the ministry reflected an inner urge and "desire to serve God and humanity." In the fall of 1947, he preached his trial sermon at Ebenezer Baptist Church and applied for admission to several theological schools. Martin Luther King, Jr., was ordained to the Baptist ministry on February 25, 1948, and was accepted in April 1948 for admission to Crozer Theological Seminary in Chester, Pennsylvania.

Crozer Seminary, located just twenty-five miles southwest of Philadelphia, was nominally a Baptist seminary but was considered theologically liberal. During his years there, Rev. Martin Luther King, Jr., became seriously engaged in intellectual and scholarly issues. Compared to Morehouse, his grades were excellent. The Crozer professor who seemed to have the greatest influence on King's theological development was George Washington Davis, who had attended Colgate-Rochester Divinity School and received his doctorate from Yale. Davis was a proponent of the religious and social ideas of Walter Rauschenbusch, one of the founders of the Social Gospel movement in the United States. A northern Baptist, Davis taught courses titled "Christian Theology for Today," "The History of Living Religions," "The Development of Christian Ideas," and "Philosophy of Religion." In the three years King studied at Crozer, he took nine courses with Professor Davis and became grounded in the social reform aspects of the Christian religion and the tenets of modern Christian liberalism.

Professor Davis also introduced King to the personalist theology of Edgar S. Brightman at Boston University. Brightman and other personalists rejected the religious ideas of neo-orthodox religious scholars, such as German theologian Karl Barth. The neo-orthodox theologians believed that because of original sin, inherited from Adam and Eve, the individual was corrupted and could never know God through reason, which had also been corrupted. Edgar Brightman argued, however, that personal awareness of God's presence in one's life was at the core of the religious experience. In an essay called "The Place of Reason and Experience in Finding God," which King wrote for George Davis's class "Christian Theology for Today," King quoted passages from Brightman's work *The Finding of God* (1938) that endorsed both the intellectual and experiential approaches for gaining knowledge of God. Reason must be used to understand and explain experiences, including religious experiences. "Carried far enough and honestly enough," wrote Brightman, "reason is one of the ways that leads man into the very presence of God."

It was also at Crozer Seminary that young Rev. King was first introduced to the teachings and nonviolent protest techniques and strategies of the Indian leader Mahatma Gandhi. In November 1949, King attended a lecture on Gandhian philosophy and practice by A. J. Muste, a militant pacifist who had opposed both world wars and was a founder of the Fellowship of Reconciliation, a pacifist organization. In the spring of 1950, Mordecai Johnson, president of Howard University and a Baptist preacher, gave a lecture at Fellowship House in Philadelphia. Johnson had visited India earlier in the year and returned with a strong belief that Gandhi's nonviolent protest tactics could be used to change the racial status quo in the United States. King attended the lecture and became fired up by Johnson's talk and immediately went out and bought "a half-dozen books on Gandhi's life and works."

Although he was only one of six African-American students at the school, in May 1950 King was elected student body president. That victory was tarnished somewhat less than a month later when King and some friends had a violent confrontation with the white owner of Mary's Cafe in Maple Shade, New Jersey. The owner, Ernest Nichols, refused to serve King, fellow Morehouse graduate and Crozer classmate Walter McCall, and their two friends Pearl E. Smith and Doris Wilson. When the four refused to leave, Nichols pulled out a gun, went outside, and fired it into the air. The four left at that point, but later filed charges against Nichols for violating the state's civil rights law. The case was subsequently dropped when all three white witnesses refused to testify on behalf of the four complainants.

During his final year at Crozer, King took courses called "American Christianity," "Religious Development of the Personality," and "Minister's Use of the Radio." He also went to Philadelphia to audit courses at the University of Pennsylvania on philosophy and the aesthetics of Immanuel Kant. In the fall of 1950, King was also assigned to a bimonthly student pastorate at the First Baptist Church of East Elmhurst in Queens, New York, under the guidance of Rev. William E. Gardner.

Despite this hectic schedule, the young King found time at night to run the streets, often with his Morehouse buddy Walter McCall. The handsome young seminarian broke the heart of more than one young lady with designs on becoming the preacher's wife, but there was one romantic encounter that had the potential to sidetrack what was then a promising professional career. King met and started dating the daughter of the white superintendent of grounds at Crozer. Rev. J. Pius Barbour, a friend of the King family, learned of the affair after the couple was seen at a Chester nightspot, and King subsequently asked Barbour to marry them. Rev. Barbour asked the young couple not to rush into anything and to consider seriously the consequences, which they did. The young woman's family decided to send her away before the end of the school year, and King was later thankful for the fatherly advice he had received from Rev. Barbour.

In all his studies and fieldwork at Crozer Seminary, King received excellent grades and on commencement day, Tuesday, May 8, 1951, the entire King family gathered at Crozer had every reason to feel proud of M.L.'s accomplishments. He received his Bachelor of Divinity degree, the Pearl Plafker Memorial Award for "Outstanding Member of the Seminary Class," and the J. Lewis Crozer Fellowship, which provided $1,200 toward graduate school. He was also chosen class valedictorian. Earlier that year King had been accepted in the Ph.D. program in Systematic Theology at Boston University's School of Theology. There he would be able to study with Edgar S. Brightman, whose theology of personalism King had found so provocative and inspirational. In *Philosophy of Religion* (1940) Brightman had written that the religious experience brought the individual into "actual and immediate relation with the divine being." King confessed in a paper discussing Brightman's work that "there have been times that I have been carried out of myself by something greater than myself, and to that something I give myself. Has this great something been God? Maybe after all I have been religious for a number of years, and am now only becoming aware of it."

circa 1955

CHAPTER TWO

WHAT SHALL I DO?

After serving as pastor-in-charge at Ebenezer Baptist Church during the summer of 1951, Rev. Martin Luther King, Jr., arrived in Boston in September driving a brand-new green Chevrolet, a graduation gift from his father. During the first semester he found a room in a boarding house at 170 St. Botolph Street, where other Boston University students were housed. During the second semester, however, a Morehouse classmate, Philip Lenud, who was a divinity student at Tufts University, rented a suite of rooms at 397 Massachusetts Avenue, and King joined him in what became their "bachelor pad." Although they resided in the heart of Boston's nightclub district, far from being "swingers," the two soon organized a Philosophical Club among African-American students attending the various colleges and universities in the area. The group would meet one or two weekends a month and discuss a paper written by one of the members. The stimulating debates and scholarly interchanges became an important part of King's intellectual life in Boston.

At the School of Theology King enrolled in courses on the philosophy of religion, formal logic, systematic theology, and one with Edgar S. Brightman on "Personalism." During the second semester, in addition to his courses at Boston University, King enrolled as a special student at Harvard University, taking a course on the history of modern philosophy. Rev. Martin Luther King, Sr., was very concerned about his son's life in the North, and hoped that he would not succumb to "earthly temptations." But M.L. was already becoming bored with bachelor life and was really interested in settling down with the right woman. When he expressed this wish to a married friend named Mary Powell, she suggested that M.L. meet Coretta Scott, who was "really a nice girl—pretty and intelligent" although she was not overly involved in the church. M.L. thought that a plus, and asked for Coretta's telephone number.

Coretta Scott was born on April 27, 1927, on her family's farm in Perry County, twelve miles outside Marion, Alabama. Coretta was the second child born to Obie Leonard and Edythe McMurry Scott, who owned their farm. For many years, particularly during the early years of the depression, her father had had to work away from home in the local sawmill. This meant that Coretta, her mother, older sister Edythe, and younger brother Obie Jr. took care of the farm. Coretta's father saved the money from his job at the sawmill. He was quite successful and soon had three trucks and employees.

Coretta's mother enrolled Edythe and Coretta, and later their brother, Obie Jr., in the Lincoln School, a semiprivate institution in Marion, Alabama, founded after the Civil War by the American Missionary Association. The staff was integrated

Coretta Scott King and Martin Luther King, Jr., circa 1962.

and the northern white teachers at Lincoln were shunned by the southern whites. Although tuition was a financial strain on the family, they understood and deeply appreciated the value of education. Coretta sang with the choruses and received voice lessons; she learned to play the flutophone, trumpet, and piano. At fifteen, she was asked to be the director of the Junior Choir at her church, Mt. Tabor A.M.E. Zion, where her grandfather Martin McMurry was the head deacon.

By the early 1940s Obie Scott's business was prospering and the family moved into a larger home. The poor whites in the area had become jealous of his success, and on Thanksgiving, 1942, the Scott family home was burned down. Although the fire was suspicious, the authorities never investigated. "Really no one cared about what happened to black people." Her father was not discouraged and was soon able to purchase a sawmill of his own. Within two weeks a white logger working there asked to purchase it, but her father would not sell. Days later, the mill was burned down. Some friendly white people suggested that he seek an investigation, but he knew it would be of no use, and went back to work hauling other people's lumber. "He never became bitter, despite all these incidents, all the humiliations and harassment by the whites who wanted to keep him down." Coretta believed that "his example helped me not to hate; that, and my own deep belief in Christian principles."

Edythe Scott graduated from the Lincoln School in June 1943 at the top of her class and in the summer of 1943 became the first black student enrolled at Antioch College in Ohio. Despite the problems she had as the only black student at the school, Edythe encouraged her sister to apply as well when Coretta graduated from Lincoln as class valedictorian in June 1945. Coretta joined her sister at Antioch in the fall of 1945.

Although Coretta was happy and excited about attending college in the North, she soon realized that despite the quality of the schooling at the Lincoln School, she was behind her classmates academically. As a result, she became something of a grind. Her first major racial incident came in her second semester, when the Yellow Springs, Ohio, School Board refused to allow her to do her practice teaching in the public elementary schools. Antioch was a progressive, experimental college, known for its liberal policies and practices. When Coretta protested the decision, she thought the college administrators would support her. They did not, and suggested that she do her practice teaching in the all-black schools in Xenia, Ohio. Coretta refused; "I will not go to Xenia," she told the college president, "because I came here from Alabama to be free of segregation."

Coretta did her practice teaching at the school on campus, but she was very upset and disillusioned. The course of study at Antioch took six years, and as Coretta approached graduation she applied to the Juilliard School in New York City and the New England Conservatory of Music in Boston. Coretta was accepted in 1951 at the New England Conservatory, which she really preferred, and was awarded a $650 grant from the Jessie Noyes Smith Foundation.

After a late start in Boston, Coretta had settled into a regular routine of study and work when she received a call from Martin Luther King, Jr., in February 1952. Earlier, Mary Powell had asked Coretta whether or not she had ever heard of Martin Luther King, Jr. She had not, so Mary described him. When Mary mentioned that he was a Baptist minister, this was a turnoff for Coretta. "I began to think of stereotypes of ministers I had known—fundamentalists in their thinking, very narrow, and overly pious," she later recalled.

Coretta agreed to meet him for lunch the next day, and despite her first impression that he was short and unimpressive, she came to realize how charming, eloquent, and sincere he was, even though he was still very young. He seemed to know exactly what he wanted and where he was headed.

When they got back to the conservatory, M.L. told her seriously, "You know, you have everything I have ever wanted in a wife. There are only four things and you have them all." Coretta asked what they were. "The four things that I look for in a wife are character, intelligence, personality, and beauty. And you have them all. I want to see you again. When can I?" Coretta, trying to maintain her composure, said she'd check her schedule, but he could call her. After he left, Coretta thought it seemed strange that he was talking about marriage on their first date. She liked him, but she would keep her defenses up; "I did not want anything to stop me, to stop my career."

M.L. called the next day, and soon the couple began to see each other constantly. The only major problem seemed to be Coretta's career plans. M.L. believed in women's equality, but he also made it clear that he expected his wife to be his partner and to be at home when he arrived. "I will be pastor of a large Negro church in the South," he told her, and he wanted a wife who would be at home in that world. Gradually, Coretta realized that she was falling in love with "Martin" (as she came to call him) and that if she was going to marry him, she would have to accept his views on her role.

Coretta's first encounter with the King family was "not an unqualified success," according to her, but when M.L. told his father that he wanted to marry Coretta, Daddy King realized "that it was real between them, and that no amount of discouragement was going to mean anything at all. And so I reluctantly agreed that they should marry."

The wedding took place on June 18, 1953, outside Marion, Alabama, at the newly built home of Obie and Edythe Scott. All of the King family was there, as well as members of Ebenezer and selected friends from Atlanta. Coretta preferred a small private wedding rather than a large public affair, and Rev. Martin Luther King, Sr., performed the service with Edythe, Coretta's sister, as maid of honor, and A. D. King as M.L.'s best man. After a brief reception, the couple drove into Marion and stayed at the home of Mr. and Mrs. Robert Tubbs, friends of the family. Robert Tubbs was the Scott family's undertaker, and M.L. often teased Coretta about the fact that "we spent our honeymoon in a funeral parlor." Later that week, they all returned to Atlanta and the Kings gave the newlyweds a reception at their home for friends. That Sunday, M.L. preached at Ebenezer and Coretta officially joined the church. The following day, Coretta began a job as a clerk in the Atlanta Citizens' Trust Company, where Daddy King was a director, and the couple remained in Atlanta for the remainder of the summer.

When Martin Luther and Coretta Scott King returned to Boston in September 1953, they took an apartment at 396 Northhampton Street. This was Coretta's last year at the conservatory and she had a very hectic schedule, especially since she had switched her major to music education. King had finished his course work and residency requirement at Boston University, and now had to concentrate on his four qualifying examinations for the doctorate and the dissertation topic. By the end of December 1953, King had completed three of his qualifying examinations; and had also begun working on the outline for his dissertation. King's topic was "A Comparison of the Conception of God in the Thinking of Paul Tillich and Henry Nelson Wieman."

Paul Johannes Tillich (1886–1965) was a German theologian forced to flee his homeland in 1933 by the Nazis because of his association with religious socialists. He came to the United States and taught at Union Theological Seminary in New York City until 1954, when he accepted a position at Harvard University. In his writings Tillich emphasized the oneness of God or "monism" and God's transcendence or existence outside of all things. Henry Nelson Wieman (1884–1975) served as a Presbyterian minister before attending Harvard University. He taught at Occidental College, the University of

Chicago, and several other universities. In his books and essays, Wieman argued in favor of God's immanence, or presence in all things, a "pluralist" position. Both Tillich and Wieman opposed the views of the "personalists," such as Edgar Brightman and George Davis, who emphasized God's personality and described him in anthropocentric terms. In a 1940 essay "The Idea of A Personal God," for example, Tillich wrote that "to speak of God as a person would mean making him an object besides other objects, a being among beings, maybe the highest, but anyhow a being." Such a view Tillich considered "a form of blasphemy."

King's advisor, L. Harold DeWolf, thought a comparison of Tillich and Weiman's writings an excellent dissertation topic and urged King to proceed with his research. DeWolf and the second reader for the dissertation, S. Paul Schilling, were impressed with King's performance in their classes and on the qualifying examinations. Both believed King would have little difficulty completing the study. Historians have since unearthed King's tendency in the dissertation and in his academic papers to appropriate without attribution the words of individuals he was discussing. During his lifetime, King's plagiarisms went undetected. When S. Paul Schilling was later informed of it, he conceded that King was "guilty of shoddy scholarship," but ultimately concluded that "his appropriation of the language of others does not entail inaccurate interpretation of the thought of the writers cited."

Indeed, it was fairly clear that King's views on these theologians were consistent in all his papers and in the dissertation. He rejected Wieman's pluralism and the monism of Tillich in favor of a broad vision of a single deity. In his overall assessment of the completed dissertation, Schilling found that "the comparisons and evaluations are fair-minded, balanced, and cogent. [King] shows sound comprehension and critical capacity."

King's last qualifying examination was completed successfully in February 1954. Before submitting his dissertation outline, which was approved in April 1954, King decided to look for a job. He had been recommended for several academic positions, but he decided he would prefer to seek the pastorate of a black church in the South. With that in mind, King accepted an invitation to speak at Dexter Avenue Baptist Church in Montgomery, Alabama. A small church of less than four hundred members, its congregation was made up of mostly middle-class and professional blacks, many of whom worked at Alabama State College, the black college located in Montgomery. The previous minister, Rev. Vernon Johns, was highly educated and well known throughout the country, but had resigned abruptly because church leaders failed to support his militant stances on civil rights issues. Although he had delivered numerous sermons before, when King visited Dexter Avenue Baptist Church, he was very conscious that this time he was being tested.

On January 24, 1954, King delivered his trial sermon, "The Three Dimensions of a Complete Life,"at Dexter. The text was taken from Revelation 21:16, "The length and the breadth and the height of it are equal," referring to St. John's vision of "a new and holy Jerusalem descending out of heaven from God." The first dimension of a complete life is the development of one's inner powers; the second dimension is the development of concern for one's fellow man; the third dimension is to seek the knowledge of God. The Dexter congregation was very impressed with the young minister and later the pulpit committee voted unanimously to call him to the pastorate. When Rev. King assured them that he planned to stay and had no

◆ REV. VERNON JOHNS ◆

Rev. Vernon Johns was a legendary and controversial figure before he was called to the pastorate of Dexter Avenue Baptist Church. Highly educated and considered a brilliant preacher, Johns had pastored several historic churches in various parts of the South and served as president of Virginia Baptist Seminary in Petersburg. When he arrived at Dexter in 1949, Rev. Johns refused to submit to the indignities associated with the Jim Crow system, and urged his parishioners to do the same. When Dexter's Board of Deacons did not go along with proposals for militant defiance of white supremacist practices, Rev. Johns would submit his resignation. The Dexter Board refused to accept Rev. Johns's resignation on at least four occasions.

When a young black man was shot down in broad daylight near Dexter, the local police made no attempt to arrest the white man everyone suspected of the crime. Johns was outraged and announced on the church bulletin board the topic for his sermon the following Sunday: IT IS SAFE TO KILL NEGROES IN MONTGOMERY. An all-white Grand Jury decided to charge Johns with inciting to riot and subpoenaed him to appear before it to show cause why he should not be indicted. The dignified and thoughtful Johns told the Grand Jury that until the police made an arrest, the topic of his sermon was merely a statement of fact. Johns was dismissed by the Grand Jury and he preached his sermon.

Johns believed that the black community should be economically self-sufficient and should not patronize white businesses that did not treat them with respect. When Johns began raising his own fruits and vegetables and selling them at a stand in front of the church, the members of his socially elite congregation were embarrassed and requested that he close it down. Johns refused and again submitted his resignation. To his shock and surprise this time the Board of Deacons decided to accept. Johns tried to withdraw his letter of resignation (he had not really planned to leave), but the Board decided to declare the pulpit vacant. Johns remained in the parsonage for several months, but decided to return to Petersburg where his wife, Alternate Johns, was on the faculty at Virginia State College. After leaving Montgomery, Rev. Johns was invited to preach at churches and schools throughout the country. He died in 1965.

intention of seeking a teaching position, they offered him the highest salary of any black minister in Montgomery.

After finalizing the details in Montgomery in April 1954, King returned to Boston enthusiastic about his future prospects. Coretta, on the other hand, had strong misgivings. She enjoyed the freedom she had experienced living in the North. Coretta had been raised just eighty miles from Montgomery and knew the situation there all too well. She also felt it would make her career in music extremely difficult to pursue. But she eventually agreed to the move because "it was an inevitable part of a greater plan for our lives."

Because there was no regular minister at Dexter Avenue Baptist Church, King traveled back and forth between Montgomery and Boston throughout the summer of 1954. Martin and Coretta moved into the church's parsonage at 309 South Jackson Street at the end of September. The new minister plunged right into his pastoral duties. In addition to conducting Sunday services, Rev. King had to visit the sick, provide food and other assistance for the needy, oversee the various educational programs, and travel to denominational meetings and conventions. He continued to accept invitations to preach in churches of friends and colleagues in Atlanta, Philadelphia, Detroit, and other places. Despite his many absences and hectic schedule, his parishioners adored him and supported him wholeheartedly when he undertook an extensive social and political action program.

On May 17, 1954, the U.S. Supreme Court rendered one of its most important decisions. The Court ruled unanimously in *Brown v. Topeka Board of Education* that "separate but equal" public educational facilities were inherently unequal. Basing their ruling on the Fourteenth Amendment to the Constitution, the justices declared that legal segregation of the races in public education was a denial of "equal protection of the law" to black children who were stigmatized and burdened with a "badge of inferiority" in the separate public schools. Black Americans across the country were jubilant over the Court's ruling and considered this the beginning of the end of their second-class status in American society.

From the outset, most southern whites denounced the Supreme Court's decision. Southern politicians vowed to do everything in their power to overturn the Court's decision, and for those who sought to end the legal separation of the races, they promised to engage in "massive resistance." The *Brown* decision spawned a social movement at the grassroots level that would oppose the NAACP and other groups' attempts to desegregate southern public schools. In Indianola, Mississippi, in July 1954, the first "White Citizens Council" (WCC) was formed and the group spread quickly throughout the region. By October 1954 WCC leaders claimed to have over 80,000 members in the state of Mississippi alone. One of the group's major objectives was the passage of a constitutional amendment that would set aside the Supreme Court's *Brown* decision.

By the beginning of the 1954–55 school year, the desegregation movement had begun. Public school officials in several border states and the District of Columbia began the process of school desegregation. NAACP officials held meetings with leaders from branches in the deep South states to provide them with information about how to petition local school administrators to force them to develop plans for integrating public schools.

King became involved in NAACP activities in Montgomery through the encouragement of another young Baptist minister, Rev. Ralph David Abernathy, who became King's closest friend. Abernathy first met Rev. Martin Luther King, Jr., in

Atlanta in 1950 when Abernathy went to hear King preach one Sunday at Ebenezer Baptist Church. Abernathy, then a graduate student at Atlanta University, recalled that "I sat there burning with envy at his learning and confidence. Already he was a scholar, and while he didn't holler as loud as some of the more famous preachers I had heard, he could holler loud enough when he wanted to. Even then I could tell that he was a man with a special gift from God." Abernathy introduced himself to King after the service, but their next meeting a few days later was quite awkward. Abernathy had been pursuing a young woman at the time who seemed not too interested in him. She had agreed to go with him to a choir recital on the Atlanta University campus, but on the day of the concert she called and said she had a terrible cold. Abernathy decided to go to the concert alone, but when he arrived, he found the woman there on the arm of Rev. Martin Luther King, Jr. When Abernathy went to speak to King, the woman tried to duck behind King's back. As they talked, she crouched behind King, "twisting his arm as if she were trying to tear it out of its socket." Abernathy decided not to make the situation any more uncomfortable and left the two alone.

After a year at Atlanta University, Abernathy returned to Montgomery and took a position at Alabama State College as dean of men. While still in training and serving as the acting pastor of First Baptist Church, one of the oldest and most prestigious black churches in the city, Abernathy was called to its pulpit in 1952. He was only twenty-six years old. By the time Martin Luther King, Jr., arrived in Montgomery, Abernathy had established himself as one of the leading black ministers in the city and was active in political affairs and able to introduce King to many circles. In January 1955, Abernathy convinced the leaders of the NAACP to allow Rev.

King to deliver the installation address for the branch officers and executive committee.

King's Ph.D. was conferred in absentia at the Boston University commencement on June 5, 1955. The Kings were doubly excited in the spring of 1955 because Coretta announced to Martin that he was going to become a father. The couple's first of four children, a girl, was born on November 17, 1955. They named her Yolanda Denise and called her "Yoki."

By the end of 1955 King had become thoroughly immersed in political activities in Montgomery, and more and more involved in the local NAACP. After appearing as the featured speaker at NAACP mass rallies and meetings, King was asked in August 1955 to join the branch's executive committee. At

Coretta, Yoki, and Martin, circa 1955.

the time, the excutive committee was preparing a petition calling on local school officials to desegregate the public schools. King also became active in the NAACP's attempts to end the discriminatory practices of the local public transit company. In Montgomery (and other southern cities and towns at that time) black passengers were legally forced to sit in the back of the bus. Not only that, but the white drivers often insulted and abused them, especially the black women. Blacks made up over 70 percent of the bus riders and often protested their treatment to company officials, to no avail. In 1955, three black passengers were arrested and charged with disorderly conduct when they each refused to give up their seats to white passengers. Rev. King was a member of the committee that protested the arrest of fifteen-year-old Claudette Colvin in March 1955 for disorderly conduct after she refused to give up her seat in the rear of the bus to a white passenger. Again nothing was done.

E. D. Nixon, an officer in the Montgomery NAACP chapter, was interested in finding a test case to challenge in the courts the bus company's practices. However, he did not believe that Colvin's arrest was a suitable incident because the teenager was unmarried and several months pregnant. But when Rosa Parks was arrested after refusing to give up her seat to a white passenger, Nixon thought that this could be the incident around which to rally the entire black community.

circa 1956

CHAPTER THREE

OH, WASN'T THAT A DAY

---◆---

People always say that I didn't give up my seat because I was tired, but that isn't true." In her 1992 autobiography, Rosa Parks set the historical record straight. "I was not tired physically, or no more tired than I usually was at the end of a working day. I was not old, although some people have that image of me being old then. I was forty-two. No, the only tired I was, was tired of giving in." In December 1955, Rosa Parks was working as an assistant tailor in the Montgomery Fair Department Store, but she had been active in civil rights organizations in the city for over a decade. Rosa Parks's courageous act of resistance set the stage for the rise to national leadership by the twenty-six-year-old pastor of Dexter Avenue Baptist Church, Rev. Martin Luther King, Jr.

Rosa Parks became involved in the Montgomery NAACP's voter registration campaign in 1943. After several unsuccessful attempts to pass the "literacy test" used to disqualify most black southerners, "I got registered in 1945 when I was thirty-two years old, so I had to pay $1.50 [poll tax] for each of the eleven years between the time I was twenty-one and the time I was thirty-two. At that time $16.50 was a considerable amount of money." In 1943, Rosa Parks became secretary of the Montgomery NAACP. She worked closely with E. D. Nixon and kept notes on the organization's legal activities between 1945 and 1950. In 1954, Parks met and began to work for Virginia Durr and her husband, attorney Clifford Durr, a liberal white couple who became actively involved in the civil rights struggles. In the summer of 1955, Virginia Durr made arrangements for Parks to attend a ten-day workshop, "Racial Desegregation: Implementing the Supreme Court Decision," held at the Highlander Folk School in Monteagle, Tennessee, which sponsored workshops on race relations, workers' rights, and labor relations, and trained future leaders for social change.

On Thursday evening, December 1, 1955, on her way home from work, Rosa Parks was arrested by two policemen after she refused to move when the white bus driver ordered her to give up her bus seat to a standing white passenger. The policemen took her to City Hall and began asking her questions and filling out the legal forms. They did not allow her to make a telephone call. The officers then took her to the city jail, where they confiscated her personal items, took a mug shot, fingerprinted her, and placed her in a cell. Parks again asked to use the telephone, and after the matron got permission from her superiors, she called her husband, Raymond, who was very upset and said he would be there right away.

Word of Parks's arrest spread rapidly in the black community. E. D. Nixon called the jail to find out the charges, but the authorities would not explain. He then called Clifford Durr,

E. D. Nixon, left, and Rosa Parks, center, after her trial.

who called the police and was told she had been arrested for violating the segregation laws. Raymond Parks, Nixon, and the Durrs went to the city jail. Nixon signed for Rosa's bond, and the trial was set for Monday, December 5. When she arrived home at about 9:30 that evening, Rosa was tired and hungry, but surrounded by family and friends. E. D. Nixon asked her if she was willing to let her arrest be the test case to challenge the bus segregation laws. After discussing it with her husband, she agreed.

Rev. Martin Luther King, Jr., received a telephone call the following morning from E. D. Nixon, who described what had happened to Rosa Parks. Nixon had also discussed the matter with Rev. Ralph Abernathy and all three agreed that a boycott was the best course of action. They began contacting all of the black ministers in the city for a meeting that evening at which they would plan their strategy.

At 7:30 Friday evening, more than forty people met at Dexter

Avenue Baptist Church and had a lively discussion about the ramifications of a bus boycott. Finally, it was agreed that a one-day protest would take place on Monday, December 5, and a citywide mass rally would be held at Holt Street Baptist Church that evening to plan the next steps. Rev. King was appointed to the committee that would prepare the leaflets announcing the boycott and mass meeting. The group also decided to contact the black taxicab companies in the city and ask the owners to charge passengers the same price as the buses on the day of the boycott.

On Saturday morning, the secretary of the Dexter Avenue Church copied 7,000 leaflets to be distributed by women and young people. King was concerned about how to inform people, but on Saturday morning he was pleasantly surprised to find that the lead story in the *Montgomery Advertiser* was about the boycott. "It appears that the *Advertiser* printed the story in order to let the white community know what the Negroes were up to; it served to bring the information to hundreds [of Negroes] who had not previously heard of the plan." News about the boycott was also disseminated from church pulpits on Sunday morning. On Monday, Martin and Coretta rose early to see the results. As the first bus passed their home, Coretta looked out of the window and shouted, "Martin, Martin, come quickly!" He ran to the window and they both watched as the bus passed with not one passenger on it.

Every bus that passed that morning was empty, and when Martin drove over and picked up Ralph Abernathy, they cruised around the city, and found it was the same everywhere. Black people were walking, thumbing rides, or piling into cars and taxicabs. None was riding the city buses. When King and Abernathy arrived at the courthouse for Rosa Parks's trial, there were over two hundred people already there. Court convened at 9:00 and it was all over in a few minutes. Parks's attorneys, Fred Gray and Charles Langford, entered a plea of "not guilty," but she was found guilty of violating the state's segregation laws and given a suspended sentence. She was fined $10, plus $4 court costs.

Around 3:00 Monday afternoon, the black ministers who had called the mass rally met at Holt Street Baptist Church to go over plans for the rally that evening. Everyone was pleased about the tremendous success of the boycott, and agreed to form an ad hoc organization to coordinate future actions. But what would the organization be called? Someone suggested the "Negro Citizens Committee," but that suggestion was rejected because the ministers did not want to limit the organization to members of the black community. Finally, Ralph Abernathy came up with the "Montgomery Improvement Association" (MIA). "Everyone paused, thought about it for a moment, and agreed that it would serve quite well."

When it came time to choose officers for the new group, the chairman, Rev. L. Roy Bennett, pastor of Holt Street Baptist Church, opened the nominations for president. Rufus Lewis, a well-respected businessman, rose and nominated Rev. M. L. King. When Lewis asked King if he would accept the nomination, King was quite surprised and hesitated for a moment. King then answered "Well, if you think I can render some service, I will." The motion was seconded and King was unanimously elected president of the MIA.

Historians have suggested several reasons for twenty-six-year-old Martin Luther King, Jr.'s election. King was a new arrival in Montgomery and had made some friends, but had no enemies in the black leadership. King was also new to white city officials who tried to make sure that they exercised a degree of control over black leaders. As Rosa Parks noted, other black leaders "had accepted favors from white people and didn't want to offend them."

King arrived home at 6:30. He had about twenty minutes to prepare his speech, but soon panicked over the thought of meeting the press. King prayed for God's guidance and inspiration, and started going over in his mind what he would say. Soon his time was up; he said goodbye to Coretta, and headed for Holt Street Baptist Church.

Because of the amount of traffic near the church, King parked several blocks away and walked. Because there were so many people in front of the church, he had to push his way to the pastor's study. The church had been packed since 5:00 P.M. and King knew that the protest was already a success. The program began with "Onward, Christian Soldiers." A prayer and a reading from the Bible followed. Then King was introduced. Speaking without notes, King made it clear that the protesters' actions were just and important for the maintenance of their self-respect and dignity as children of God, and that unlike the violence and lawlessness of the Ku Klux Klan and White Citizens Councils, "We will be guided by the highest principles of law and order." King emphasized that the protest would be guided by "the doctrine of Christian love." "Our method will be that of persuasion, not coercion. . . . Love must be our regulating ideal."

The applause from the assembled crowd was thunderous when he finished. King knew that he had struck the right chords with his audience. After an appearance by Rosa Parks, Rev. Abernathy came forward and read the resolution. There were three demands. Black citizens would return to the buses only after the company officials agreed 1) to guarantee the courteous treatment by all bus operators, 2) to seat all passengers on a first come, first serve basis with blacks being seated back to front, and whites sitting front to back, and 3) to employ black bus operators on routes in predominantly black neighborhoods. Those assembled were asked to stand if they agreed with the demands in the resolution. A few rose at first, then more and more, until everyone in the church was standing.

King, Abernathy, attorney Fred Gray, and several others met with three city commissioners and bus company officials on Thursday, December 8, and presented the MIA's demands. The white officials refused to agree to any of the demands, and one even mentioned in passing that taxicab drivers were required to charge a minimum fee of forty-five cents per ride. The next day the police commissioner issued an order that taxicab drivers must charge the minimum fare. At the next mass meeting, volunteers were solicited to provide rides to those who needed transportation. Within days a "motor pool" system was put in place, and a list containing the forty-eight dispatch and forty-two pickup stations throughout the black community had been distributed. Eventually, a fleet of 15 new station wagons was purchased to help transport up to 30,000 black protesters each day.

❧ ❧ ❧

"Stand up for justice."

As the boycott extended into its second and third weeks, it became clear that the MIA would need more money than what was collected at the biweekly rallies for necessities such as an office and full-time staff. Unfortunately, the MIA was forced out of its first two offices when whites learned where the group was housed. Finally, the MIA rented offices in the building owned by the Bricklayer's Union, a primarily black union.

Because of the news coverage the boycott received nationally and internationally, contributions began flowing in to the MIA by the middle of December. This money was helpful, but the publicity only stiffened opposition in the white community. Many whites were adversely affected by the boycott. The bus company and downtown businesses suffered greatly, and when negotiations between MIA and city representatives broke down at the end of December, the white businessmen decided to act on their own. There were two meetings between MIA representatives and the "Men of Montgomery," a white businessmen's group, but Mayor W. A. Gayle and other city officials would not budge in their opposition to the MIA demands.

In an attempt to divide the protest movement, white leaders began circulating rumors in the black community at the beginning of January 1956 that King and other leaders were pocketing the money contributed to the MIA. Prominent white citizens also suggested that the older black leaders should be calling the shots and asked why those older leaders were taking orders from these "militant young upstarts" who, the whites argued, were blocking a solution to the problem. After hearing this complaint several times, King called a meeting of the MIA executive committee and offered his resignation. But the MIA officers gave King a unanimous vote of confidence, and made it clear that they were quite pleased with the leadership King was providing.

Then on Sunday, January 22, 1956, the local newspaper announced that the city commissioners had reached a settlement with a group of "prominent Negro ministers." Journalist Carl Rowan, who had been covering the boycott for the *Minneapolis Tribune*, got the story from the Associated Press on Saturday night before it was published and called King to verify it. King told him there had been no settlement and he had no idea who the "three prominent Negro ministers" were.

King called a meeting of the MIA leaders at ten o'clock Saturday night and they decided to call all the ministers so that they could announce in their churches that the protest was still on. Then they made the rounds of Montgomery's nightspots to spread the word. It worked, and on Sunday morning the buses were still empty. It was later revealed that the city commissioners had lured three ministers to their offices under false pretenses and claimed that they agreed to a settlement. Those ministers publicly repudiated the announcement.

From the beginning, threats and intimidation were used to keep black citizens of Montgomery from participating in the bus boycott. Raymond Parks resigned his barber's job at Maxwell Air Force Base when his employer told him "there would be no discussion of the bus protest or Rosa Parks in this establishment." Rosa Parks lost her job as a seamstress at the Montgomery Fair Department Store when they suddenly decided to close the tailoring shop. Parks, King, Abernathy, and other MIA leaders received telephone threats regularly, and the police increased their harassment of Montgomery's black community after the city commissioners' phony "settlement" was exposed.

In late January 1956, when King was driving some people home from a shopping center, he was followed by the police, pulled over, and arrested for traveling thirty miles an hour in a twenty-five miles per hour zone. When the policemen took him away, he told the passengers, Robert Williams and Lillie Thomas, to notify Coretta at once. King was understandably fearful for his personal safety, but felt relieved when he realized he was being taken to the Montgomery city jail. After being held in a crowded cell, he was ushered into another room and fingerprinted.

News of King's arrest spread quickly, and a large crowd

formed outside the station. Soon Rev. Abernathy arrived to post bond, but had to leave to collect more money when he was told that the only way King would be released that night was with a cash bond. The crowd inside and outside the jail grew larger and larger. Finally the jailer panicked, rushed into the finger-printing room, and released King. After returning his personal belongings, the jailer told King he was released on his own bond and his trial would take place Monday morning at 8:30.

The night before his trial, King received a series of tele-phone threats. He later recalled sitting at the kitchen table thinking about his young daughter and "how she could be taken from me at any time." King sat there, praying for strength to handle this ordeal, when suddenly he heard an inner voice. "Martin Luther, stand up for righteousness. Stand up for justice. Stand up for truth. And lo I will be with you, even until the end of the world." King believed he had heard the voice of Jesus Christ, and it gave him the strength and courage to go on. "Almost at once my fears began to go. My uncertainty disappeared." The following morning he went to the courthouse spiritually rejuvenated and was, of course, found guilty of "speeding." He paid the $10 fine, and $4 court costs, and his lawyer, Fred Gray, filed an appeal.

The vicious telephone threats continued. King decided that he did not want Coretta to be alone when he was away from home. On January 30, 1956, King went to the MIA's regular Monday evening mass meeting at First Baptist Church, and Coretta and a fellow church member, Mary Lucy Williams, remained at the King home. At about 9:30 the two were talk-ing in the sitting room when Coretta heard a heavy thump on the front porch. Given the threats, she and Mary Lucy went toward the back of the house where Yoki was sleeping. As they were moving, "there was a thunderous blast. Then smoke and the sound of breaking glass. Mary Lucy grabbed me and started crying. Her screaming frightened me, and I was shaken by the impact and the noise." They made it to Yoki, who was fine. Then they heard the doorbell. "Who is it?" Coretta shouted. She heard the voices of their neighbors and opened the door. The windows in the front of the house were blown out; glass was everywhere. The concrete porch was split, and there was a small hole where the bomb had exploded.

Ralph Abernathy received news of the bombing from Mary Lucy Williams's husband, Roscoe, but did not interrupt King's address. Finally, because there was so much commotion in the back of the church, King stopped and asked what happened. When he was told, King maintained his composure. Before leaving he told the audience that this was another "test of faith," but that "we cannot win this battle if we respond to violence by retaliating. . . . An eye for an eye and a tooth for a tooth will only end up in a blind generation and a toothless people."

When King arrived at his home, he found a huge crowd in front of it. Mayor Gayle, Police Commissioner Clyde Sellers, and several white reporters who were waiting inside expressed their regrets about the incident, but the crowd outside was becoming angry. The atmosphere was tense. King stepped onto the porch and asked for quiet. He assured them that his family was fine and cautioned the members of the crowd against any type of "retaliatory violence." In a speech that was recorded by the television cameras present, King urged them "to meet violence with nonviolence. . . . We must love our white brothers no matter what they do to us. We must make them know that we love them. . . ."

When the police commissioner began to address the crowd, there were loud boos. King returned to the porch and asked the crowd to listen to the commissioner, who offered a reward for information about the perpetrators of the crime. The crowd dispersed and violence was averted. Two days later, when two sticks of dynamite exploded on the lawn of E. D. Nixon's home, another large crowd gathered. Again there was no violence.

❧ ❧ ❧

"Proud to be arrested"

After threats, intimidation, and violence had failed, city officials decided to use an old anti-boycott statute to indict the leaders of the bus protest. On Sunday, February 21, 1956, the *Advertiser* published the names of those who were to be arrested for calling the boycott. The following morning the police began showing up at people's homes and taking them away. Ralph Abernathy recalled that after he was arrested and taken to the city jail, "it turned out that everybody who was anybody in the black community had been arrested that day." After being photographed and fingerprinted, Abernathy paid his bond and left with others who had been arrested.

King was in Nashville, Tennessee, lecturing at Fisk University, when he learned of the indictments. He cut his engagement short and flew to Atlanta, where Coretta and Yoki were with his parents. Daddy King was growing increasingly concerned about his son's family's safety, and when he could not convince them to stay in Atlanta, he decided to accompany them back to Montgomery the next day. Reporters crowded around the car as soon as they entered Montgomery. When King arrived home, Abernathy came by, and with Daddy King, they all went to the city jail where "an almost holiday atmosphere prevailed." Some people had even rushed down to the jail to be arrested, but no one was afraid. Indeed, they were "proud to be arrested for the cause of freedom." King was charged, photographed, and fingerprinted again. After a church member paid the bond, he returned home.

The trial began on Monday, March 19, 1956, with Judge Eugene Carter presiding. The courtroom was packed with people from all over the world. King was the first of the ninety defendants. For four days witnesses for the prosecution testified that the boycott against the bus company was called for no "just cause." Witnesses for the defense testified about the way that they or members of their family had been treated (and mistreated) by bus company employees. When both sides rested their cases on Thursday, March 22, Judge Carter immediately announced his verdict: King was guilty. The judge fined King $500 and court costs, or 365 days at hard labor. The judge granted the other eighty-nine defendants a continuance pending the appeal of King's conviction.

King's lawyers not only appealed his conviction, they brought proceedings in federal court alleging that the Alabama bus segregation law violated the Fourteenth Amendment to the U.S. Constitution. After *Browder v. Gayle* was heard by a three-judge panel on May 11, 1956, they ruled, in a two-to-one decision two weeks later, that the bus segregation law was unconstitutional. The state attorneys immediately appealed the panel's decision to the United States Supreme Court.

During the late spring and summer of 1956, King made a grueling coast-to-coast speaking tour recounting "The Montgomery Story," and raising funds for the MIA. The young Baptist minister had become a national celebrity and was in great demand on the lecture circuit. However, by the early fall, the traveling and speaking had taken a heavy toll on King's health and his doctor ordered him to rest for a while.

Meanwhile, whites in powerful positions continued their

King and Ralph Abernathy being booked, February 23, 1956.

attempts to halt the bus boycott. On October 30, 1956, Montgomery mayor W. A. Gayle instructed city officials to seek an injunction against the car pool because it was a "public nuisance" and a "private enterprise" operating without a license or franchise. When federal judge Frank M. Johnson refused to grant a restraining order to keep the city from interfering with the car pool, King felt this was the beginning of the end of the protest campaign.

On Tuesday, November 13, 1956, Martin Luther King, Jr., was back in state court as the chief defendant in the city's latest legal maneuver to end the protest. King's lawyers argued that the car pool was a "share-a-ride" program provided by the black churches and was run on a nonprofit basis. During the morning recess, there was a brief commotion in the back of the courtroom. A journalist covering the trial came over and handed King a news release from the Associated Press. It read: "The United States Supreme Court today affirmed a decision of a special three-judge U.S. District Court in declaring Alabama's state and local laws requiring segregation on buses unconstitutional. The Supreme Court acted without listening to any argument; it simply said 'the motion to affirm is granted and the Judgment is affirmed.'" Presiding Judge Elmer Carter called the court to order and both sides continued with their presentations. Within five minutes of the resting of their cases, Judge Carter granted the city an injunction to halt the car pool, but the decision was anticlimatic.

Upon hearing the Court's decision, white supremacists in Montgomery threatened violence if the buses were integrated and the Ku Klux Klan staged marches in black neighborhoods. As the day for the implementation of the court order drew closer, information was distributed at mass meetings on the proper conduct on the newly integrated buses. Rev. Glenn Smiley, a white minister and founder of the Fellowship of Reconciliation, a pacifist group, and other black and white leftists offered their expertise and services to the Montgomery movement. Bayard Rustin, another militant pacifist and member of the Fellowship, was instrumental in introducing King to "philosophical pacifism" and nonviolent direct-action protest strategies and tactics. Rustin also introduced King to northern white activists and philanthropists who could support the bus protest, among them Stanley Levison, a New York attorney who had made a fortune in the garment industry in the 1940s. Levison used his considerable energies and resources to assist beleaguered leftist groups and individuals, including the Communists who came under attack during the Red Scare fomented by Wisconsin Senator Joseph McCarthy in the early 1950s. Despite the fact that Levison and Rustin were sometimes labeled Communists (an allegation which they denied), they became close and trusted advisors to King and his associates and formed the organization "In Fellowship" in New York City to raise funds for the MIA throughout the Northeast.

On Thursday, December 20, 1956, the order reached Montgomery. The next morning, with reporters and television cameras rolling, King, Rosa Parks, Abernathy, E. D. Nixon, and Glenn Smiley boarded and sat in the front of Montgomery's first integrated bus. On the whole, the first day went well; however, by the end of the month, after news reporters had left, white racists launched a reign of terror. Shots were fired at buses at night, wounding a black woman in the leg; a black teenage girl was beaten by five white men as she left a bus one evening. The city commissioners suspended bus service after 5:00 P.M. because of the violence. Then on Tuesday, January 9, 1957, while King and Abernathy were in Atlanta, Abernathy received a telephone call in the middle of the night from his wife Juanita informing him that their home had been bombed. Throughout that night they received calls from Montgomery and learned that not only Abernathy's home, but his church, First Baptist, along with three other churches—Bell, Hutchison Street, and Mt. Olive Baptist—had been bombed. The home of Rev. Robert Graetz, the white clergyman who had been a strong supporter of the bus boycott from the beginning, was also dynamited.

After the bombings, the city commissioners decided to cancel the bus company's contract and end bus service in the city altogether. At the mass meeting that following on Monday, January 15, 1957, everyone was very depressed and discouraged, especially King. It was his twenty-eighth birthday, and he prayed, "Lord, I hope no one will have to die as a result of our struggle for freedom in Montgomery. Certainly I don't want to die. But if anyone has to die, let it be me." At that point King was unable to control his emotions and he broke down in public for the first time, and was led from the pulpit by two fellow ministers.

Although daytime bus service later resumed, another wave of bombings took place on Sunday, January 28, 1957. The home of Allen Robertson, who owned the People's Cab Stand, was damaged and an unexploded bomb containing twelve sticks of dynamite was found on the porch of the Kings' home. At this point white city officials realized that the situation had gotten completely out of hand, and began offering rewards for information about the terrorists. On January 31, 1957, police officials announced that they had arrested seven white men in connection with the bombings. At the subsequent trials, despite the fact that they had signed confessions, the all-white juries found the men not guilty. After these arrests, the wave of bombings ended.

❧ ❧ ❧

"Give us the ballot. . ."

Blacks in several other southern cities began organizing Montgomery-like protests against segregation in various areas of public life. Bayard Rustin, Stanley Levison, and Ella Baker, a former field secretary for the NAACP, urged King to take the lead in the formation of a regional organization that would assist local black communities engaged in nonviolent direct-action protests against Jim Crow segregation and other forms of oppression. After King conferred with Rev. C. K. Steele in Tallahassee and Rev. Fred Shuttlesworth in Birmingham, the three clergymen sent out one hundred invitations to southern black leaders for a meeting in Atlanta on January 10–11, 1957. About sixty persons attended the meeting held at Ebenezer Baptist Church and discussed the increasing number of mass protests taking place throughout the South. The participants established the "Southern Leadership Conference on Transportation and Nonviolent Integration," and elected

Though King was convicted of leading the Montgomery boycott, his sentence was suspended.

King chairman. A follow-up meeting organized by Rustin and Baker took place in New Orleans on February 14, 1957, where the one hundred leaders in attendance agreed to form a permanent organization. The first annual conference of the "Southern Christian Leadership Conference" (SCLC) was held in Atlanta in August 1957. The title of the conference was "to redeem the soul of America," and its purpose was to support and provide assistance to nonviolent direct-action protests for social justice to black communities throughout the region.

King initially believed that SCLC would receive financial assistance from civic, religious, and labor organizations as well as philanthropic foundations; however, this did not occur, particularly in its early years. Most of its early funding came from black churches and other social organizations that made contributions in direct response to appeals from King, who was increasingly recognized as a national black leader. A. Philip Randolph and Roy Wilkins were the major organizers of the

Prayer Pilgrimage to Washington, D.C., on May 17, 1957, the third anniversary of the *Brown* decision, to demonstrate support for voting rights and the implementation of public school desegregation. King delivered his first national address at that march before an audience of 27,000. In his speech King made the denial of voting rights to southern blacks his main theme. "Give us the ballot," King declared, "and we will no longer have to worry the federal government about our rights."

In July 1957, King had received the NAACP's highest honor, the Spingarn Award, bestowed annually on an individual for his or her contributions to the improvement of race relations in the United States. Nonetheless, with the founding of SCLC, tensions developed between King and the NAACP leadership. Roy Wilkins, Thurgood Marshall, Clarence Mitchell, and other NAACP officials viewed SCLC as competition for the limited funds available to support civil rights causes. Rev. Joseph Lowery, one of SCLC's founders, recalled that when SCLC was being organized, "we met with strong opposition from the NAACP. Well, the thing got so bad, that Martin, Ralph [Abernathy], and I went to New York and had a meeting with Roy Wilkins" and other NAACP officials. King tried to placate the NAACP leaders by making sure that there would be no competition for members between the two civil rights groups. Unlike the NAACP, SCLC would accept no individual memberships. That is, groups and organizations only could become SCLC "affiliates," by paying a $25 annual fee. King also agreed to help raise money for the NAACP branches wherever he went to speak for SCLC.

The passage of the Civil Rights Act of 1957 created the U.S. Commission on Civil Rights and the Civil Rights Division within the Justice Department. In the wake of this, SCLC launched the "Crusade for Citizenship," the objective of which was to double the black vote in the South by 1960. While the NAACP focused primarily on public school desegregation in the South, SCLC would concentrate on voting rights. Beginning on Lincoln's birthday in February 1958, the Crusade for Citizenship sponsored rallies in twenty-two cities to encourage the formation of local voter-registration committees that would oversee the voting drives in each community. Ella Baker, SCLC's first associate director, set up its office in Atlanta and developed the materials distributed to local voting rights committees that joined the Crusade for Citizenship. King often spoke at these rallies and helped to raise funds to sustain the local voting rights campaigns.

Once the local registration committees were established, however, SCLC had only limited contact with and control over them. Indeed, even as King's fame grew nationally and internationally in 1958 and 1959, the SCLC and the voting rights campaign floundered. By the end of 1959 King had become aware of the organization's invisibility and admitted that "the SCLC had not been publicized through the press or otherwise.

King with A. Philip Randolph (center) and Roy Wilkins (right).

The aim and purposes of the Conference have not gotten over to a large number of people North and South." Historians have suggested that white resistance to black demands for voting rights and the absence of viable protest organizations in southern black communities, such as the Montgomery Improvement Association or Tallahassee's Inter-Civic Council, were the most important factors limiting the growth of the voting rights campaigns in the late 1950s.

❦ ❦ ❦

"*I have no choice but to free you now.*"

King traveled throughout the country at this time making speeches and raising money to get SCLC off the ground. In the middle of October 1957, he had to rush back to Atlanta because Coretta gave birth to a son, whom they named Martin Luther King III and called Little Marty. Within a few days, King was back on the road. Earlier that year the Kings had made their first trip abroad after receiving an invitation from Dr. Kwame Nkrumah, prime minister designate, to attend independence celebrations for Ghana in West Africa. In March 1957, Ghana became the first former European colony in Africa to gain independence. The Kings were part of an American delegation that included Congressman Adam Clayton Powell, UN diplomat Ralph Bunche, and Brotherhood of Sleeping Car Porters president A. Philip Randolph; and on the return trip they made stops in Nigeria, Rome, Geneva, Paris, and London. Upon his return to the United States, King spoke at the Prayer Pilgrimage in May 1957. Soon afterward, he signed a contract with Harper and Row to publish his personal account of the Montgomery bus boycott, *Stride Toward Freedom*. King was also one of the black leaders invited to the White House to meet with President Dwight D. Eisenhower in June 1958. Lester Granger of the Urban League, Wilkins, Randolph, and Powell also attended.

Less than two weeks before *Stride Toward Freedom* was to be released, however, King received another glaring reminder that despite his growing national and international recognition, he was still just another Negro in the South. On September 3, 1958, when Martin and Coretta went to the Montgomery courthouse to meet with his lawyer Fred Gray and to see Ralph Abernathy testify in a civil trial, King was ordered by a white policeman to move along. When King refused and told the white officer that he was waiting for his lawyer, the policeman responded, "If you don't get the hell out of here, you're going to need a lawyer." When King did not move, the officer and another policeman grabbed King and pushed him down the courtroom stairs and into a patrol wagon. When he was taken to the jail, a reporter there began taking photos; soon the policemen realized whom they had arrested. King was charged with disorderly conduct and resisting arrest, but since he had done nothing wrong, he refused to pay any bail.

At the trial two days later, King was found guilty by Judge Eugene Loe and fined $10 or fourteen days in jail. King asked to read a statement in which he explained why he refused to pay the fine. "The time has come when perhaps only the willing and nonviolent acts of suffering by the innocent can arouse this nation to wipe out the scourge of brutality and violence inflicted upon Negroes who seek only to walk with dignity before God and man." The judge was surprised and angry. Later, when the policemen came to take the prisoners who had been sentenced away, they would not take King. After he told

THE CIVIL RIGHTS ACT OF 1957

With the increase in the black vote in northern states in the post–World War II period, both Democratic and Republican leaders recognized the need to place civil rights high on their political agendas. In 1956, a presidential election year, liberal Democrats became interested in putting the resources of the Department of Justice behind public school desegregation efforts in the South. Legislation was introduced into Congress that would have given the U.S. attorney general the power to seek injunctions against state and local officials who attempted to thwart the implementation of court-ordered public school desegregation.

The measure made little progress in Congress in 1956, and in the presidential election Dwight Eisenhower soundly defeated Adlai Stevenson, the governor of Illinois, with the help of black voters from the North who were disappointed with Stevenson's halfhearted commitment to civil rights. In his inaugural address in January 1957, Eisenhower called for the passage of legislation to provide federal protection for voting rights, and liberal Democrats led by Minnesota Senator Hubert Humphrey pushed the measure in Congress. After Senate Majority Leader Lyndon Baines Johnson from Texas decided to give his support to some type of civil rights legislation, southern Democrats failed in their attempts to weaken the measure by adding the stipulation that individuals charged with civil rights violations be given jury trials in state courts.

The compromise measure that passed the Senate on August 29, 1957, was the first civil rights law passed in eighty-two years. It called for the creation of the Civil Rights Division within the Justice Department to be directed by an assistant attorney general, made it a federal offense to interfere with voting rights, and authorized the attorney general to prosecute voting-rights cases, as opposed to cases involving public school desegregation. Most important, the new law provided for the appointment of a bipartisan Commission on Civil Rights to investigate complaints of voting rights discrimination and make recommendations for action to the Justice Department.

the authorities he was ready to serve his sentence, they told him to leave the courthouse; someone had paid his fine. Later it was revealed that Police Commissioner Clyde Sellers had paid the fine because he was aware of the bad publicity that his department would receive when the nation learned they had jailed King again.

Stride Toward Freedom was published on September 17, 1958. The book received excellent reviews and King made several promotional appearances. On September 20, while he was autographing copies of his book at Blumstein's Department Store in Harlem, a woman approached and asked, "Are you Dr. King?" King responded, "Yes, I am." "Luther King," the woman growled in a low, menacing voice, "I've been looking for you for five years." At that point the woman pulled a letter opener from under her coat and plunged it into King's chest. There were shouts and a commotion, and someone grabbed the woman. King remained calm, and there was very little blood. An ambulance took King to an operating room at Harlem Hospital with the letter opener still sticking out of his chest. King was operated on by a team of three surgeons, led by Dr. Andre D. Maynard. When Coretta arrived the next day, Dr. Maynard told her that it was good that King had remained calm throughout the ordeal, because the knife was so close to his heart that any quick movement would have killed him.

The woman who stabbed King was later identified as Isola Curry. Mentally unstable, Curry had spent some time in mental institutions. After her arrest, officers found that she was also carrying a pistol. Curry was eventually committed to an institution for the criminally insane. King remained in the hospital and in New York City for several weeks. He had been invited to make a speaking tour of India by the Gandhi Peace Foundation, and to meet Prime Minister Jawaharlal Nehru that coming February, so when Coretta and Martin returned to Montgomery, King continued his recuperation and made plans for a long-awaited trip to India.

On February 3, 1959, Martin, Coretta, and Lawrence D. Reddick, a professor of history at Alabama State College who had just completed a biography of King, *Crusader Without Violence*, left New York City and seven days later arrived in Bombay. King was shocked by the extreme poverty that he witnessed in Bombay, worse than he had seen on his trip to Africa. In New Delhi, they visited the great shrine to Gandhi and met several Indian leaders, including Prime Minister Nehru. King was impressed by how the lower caste untouchables or "Harijans" were being integrated into Indian society after centuries of extreme discrimination by the higher caste Brahmins.

Once back in Montgomery, King was confronted by the reality of SCLC's financial trouble and its meager success in registering southern blacks to vote through the Crusade for Citizenship. He also had to confront the fact that over the previous two years he had been seriously neglecting his pastoral duties at Dexter Avenue Baptist Church. While King's accomplishments were a source of pride for the members of Dexter Avenue Baptist Church, King felt guilty about his frequent extended absences. He also knew that if SCLC was to be an important civil rights organization, he would have to be in Atlanta to oversee its operations. On November 29, 1959, King announced to the Dexter Avenue congregation that he was leaving to serve as co-pastor of Ebenezer Baptist Church, and to devote more of his time and energies to the expanding civil rights movement. "History has thrust upon me a responsibility from which I cannot turn away," King told his parishioners. "I have no choice but to free you now."

King's resignation from Dexter Avenue Baptist Church took

effect in January 1960, but even before he had moved into his new home on Johnson Avenue in Atlanta, near Ebenezer Baptist Church, the newspapers were filled with reports of the new wave of civil rights protests that began in Greensboro, North Carolina, on February 1, 1960, when four black students at North Carolina A & T College staged a sit-in at the local Woolworth's department store. With lightning speed the student sit-ins spread throughout the southeastern states, and King welcomed black and white students to the ongoing campaigns for black civil rights and equal treatment for all Americans. Within a week, sit-ins were held in five other North Carolina cities, and by the end of February 1960, student protests had taken place in Hampton, Norfolk, Richmond, and Portsmouth, Virginia; Nashville and Chattanooga, Tennessee; Lexington, Kentucky; Baltimore, Maryland; and Montgomery, Alabama.

Initially, King could provide the student protesters only with moral support, because in the third week of February 1960, he was indicted by a Montgomery grand jury on charges of falsifying his state tax returns from 1956 to 1958. King was devastated by the charges that he had pocketed money raised to support the Montgomery protests, and fell into a deep depression. When several friends came forward and volunteered to help raise funds for the legal expenses, King felt heartened, but insisted that the money raised should also be used to support the student protests and other civil rights activities. Once he began to feel better about his legal problems, King spoke out publicly in support of the student sit-ins.

Ella Baker, who was still serving as SCLC's executive director, recommended to King that he sponsor a conference that would bring together the students active in sit-in cam-

King removes his shoes prior to entering the Gandhi shrine in New Delhi.

paigns. Held at Shaw University in Raleigh, North Carolina, April 15–17, 1960, more that two hundred student activists attended the conference that led to the formation of the Student Nonviolent Coordinating Committee (SNCC). King addressed the student leaders and urged them to continue their movement because they were part of a larger movement aimed at saving the soul of America and creating the "beloved community." He also advised them to create a permanent organization that would be affiliated with SCLC. Ella Baker, however, disagreed with King's suggestion and encouraged the students to create an independent organization that the students would control. The students followed Baker's advice and, although SNCC received financial and other types of support from SCLC, it was a student-controlled organization.

In May 1960, King was back in Montgomery standing trial on the tax evasion charges. King's attorneys pointed out to the twelve white jurors that King's honesty had always been evident and these charges represented a frame-up orchestrated by state officials. To King's great surprise the jury returned with a verdict of not guilty. It was an important victory that held out the hope to King and other black leaders that justice was possible in the southern court system.

By this time the 1960 presidential elections began to dominate the national news and King was being drawn more and more into the political fray. On June 22, 1960, King met with John Fitzgerald Kennedy, the U.S. senator from Massachusetts, who was locked in a fierce struggle for the Democratic presidential nomination with the Senate majority leader Lyndon Baines Johnson from Texas. Although he found Kennedy personable, King refused to endorse him or any candidate because "I feel that someone must remain in the position of nonalignment . . ." After winning the presidential nomination, Kennedy promised to support innovative measures to bring about public school integration, but King remained skeptical of white liberals who "pay lip service to integration."

As the presidential campaign wore on, King became preoccupied with civil rights developments in Atlanta, where SNCC members planned to launch an ambitious protest campaign against segregation in local stores and restaurants. King was caught in the middle because Atlanta's older black leaders, including Daddy King, objected to these more disruptive protests, preferring to fight for desegregation in the courts. King's associates were trying to set up a meeting with Kennedy in Miami at that time and King told the students he could not participate. When the meeting with Kennedy fell through, King decided to join the student sit-ins and was arrested at Rich's Department Store on October 19, 1960. Again he refused to pay the $500 bond, and promised to "stay in jail for one year or ten years" if necessary.

circa 1960

CHAPTER FOUR

THERE IS A BALM IN GILEAD

After Martin Luther King, Jr., was arrested on October 19, 1960, in Atlanta during the SNCC-sponsored sit-in at Rich's Department Store, he decided as a matter of conscience to remain in the Fulton County jail rather than pay the bond. Atlanta mayor William Hartsfield announced on Saturday, October 22, that he had reached an agreement with the student leaders that allowed them to be released from jail. Mayor Hartsfield agreed to enter into negotiations with downtown merchants to bring about a complete end of segregation in public facilities. While the students viewed this as a victory and were released, King was still held.

Earlier, in the spring of 1960, King had been stopped by the DeKalb County Police while driving the famous Georgia writer Lillian Smith, who was white, from the Kings' home in Atlanta to Emory University Hospital, where she was undergoing treat-

King as he was being arrested at Rich's Department Store.

ment. King did not have a Georgia driver's license even though he had been living in the state for more than ninety days; the Alabama license plates on his borrowed car had expired. King received two citations, and when he appeared in the DeKalb County Court in September 1960, Judge J. Oscar Mitchell dismissed the first charge, but fined King $25 on the second, which King paid. However, on the sentencing form, which only his attorney Charles Clayton saw, King was placed on probation for one year. The form specified that the defendant "shall not violate any Federal or State penal statutes or municipal ordinances."

While King was in the Fulton County jail, police officials from DeKalb County notified the administrators that King had violated his earlier probation when he was arrested in the student sit-in in Atlanta. On Monday, October 25, King was back in Judge Mitchell's courtroom and found guilty of violating his probation. Judge Mitchell sentenced King to four months of hard labor at Reidsville State Penitentiary, and was denied bond while the case was appealed. Mitchell did agree to hear an appeal-bond argument on the following Thursday.

Coretta Scott King, who was five months pregnant with their third child, was fearful of what prison administrators would allow to happen to her husband at Reidsville, a maximum security prison. On hearing the sentence, Coretta cried in public for the first time. Before they led her husband away, he told her, "I think we must prepare ourselves for the fact that I am going to have to serve this time." The reporters present sent word of King's sentencing across the nation, and in Washington, D.C., Justice Department officials informed President Eisenhower and Vice President Richard Nixon, who was then on the road campaigning for president. Neither decided to comment on the sentence, nor did they try to contact Georgia court officials. Daddy King and Coretta decided to get in touch with some other lawyers, including Morris Abram and Harris Wofford. Abram was a well-known and respected attorney, and Wofford was a young lawyer, then working on Kennedy's campaign. Wofford was the first white student to graduate from Howard University Law School, and he and his wife, Clare, had spent time in India studying Gandhian nonviolence. The Kings had been introduced to Wofford in 1957 by Bayard Rustin, and Coretta decided to call him after King had been sentenced.

At 3:30 in the morning on Wednesday, October 27, King was awakened in his jail cell by the Fulton County police, handcuffed, and led to a police wagon. King was understandably frightened, given what had happened to other blacks in custody of the Fulton County police. They drove for three hours and finally arrived at the Reidsville Penitentiary. King later told

Yoki and Martin Luther King III (far right) welcome their father back from Reidsville.

Coretta that upon arrival at Reidsville, he was thrown into a very small cell where they kept the most hardened criminals. He was also forced to put on a prison uniform. Fortunately, the other prisoners recognized him and sent him notes saying how much they respected him and his work for civil rights.

Later that day, as Coretta was preparing to go to Morris

Abram's law office, the phone rang. The caller asked to speak to Mrs. Martin Luther King, Jr., and then asked her to "hold for Senator Kennedy" who was calling from Chicago. She waited, then she heard, "Good morning, Mrs. King. This is Senator Kennedy." They exchanged greetings, and then the senator expressed his concern over her husband's incarceration and offered whatever assistance he could to them. Coretta thanked him for his thoughts and his offer.

Although Robert F. Kennedy, the senator's brother and his top campaign strategist, was at first upset when he learned of the telephone call (he thought it might alienate southern white Democrats), he was more disturbed by Judge Mitchell's harsh sentence. Robert Kennedy left Chicago for New York City and when he arrived he decided to call Judge Mitchell. Kennedy identified himself and discussed with Judge Mitchell—lawyer to lawyer—the propriety of allowing King to be released on bond pending his appeal. The next morning King's attorney, Donald L. Hollowell, went before Judge Mitchell and argued for King's release. This time the Judge agreed: King would be released on $2,000 bond pending resolution of the appeal. Hollowell chartered a plane to Reidsville, and brought King back the next day. Coretta, Christine, and A. D. King and a small crowd of people met the plane at the airport. King told the waiting reporters that he was "deeply indebted to Senator Kennedy" for his release. At a celebration and rally held at Ebenezer Baptist Church later that night, Daddy King, a long-time Republican, told the audience, "If I had a suitcase full of votes, I'd dump as many of them as he could hold right in John Kennedy's lap."

Kennedy's intervention on King's behalf occurred just days before the election, and Kennedy's campaign staff designed a small flyer that read: "No Comment Nixon versus a Candidate with a Heart, Senator Kennedy: The Case of Martin Luther King." The staff printed hundreds of thousands of the flyers and distributed them in black voting districts across the country. Historians now believe that given the narrowness of Kennedy's victory—less than 125,000 votes out of a total of 68 million cast—it was the huge black turnout, voting overwhelmingly Democratic, that allowed Kennedy to carry several large northern and midwestern states, and thus win the presidency.

❦ ❦ ❦

"Don't get weary."

In May 1961, James Farmer, one of the founders of the Congress of Racial Equality (CORE) and its current chairman, contacted King and announced that the group was launching the "Freedom Rides" across the South to challenge segregation in interstate transportation. Farmer later explained that they knew that bigoted whites would attempt to stop them. With great fanfare and publicity, interracial groups of SNCC and CORE members left Washington, D.C., on May 4, 1961. When they reached Atlanta, King and the new executive director of SCLC, Rev. Wyatt T. Walker, hosted a dinner for the Freedom Riders and wished them well on the next leg of their trip. On Sunday, May 14, 1961, when the two buses carrying the Freedom Riders reached Anniston, Alabama, the first one was attacked by a white mob. The passengers narrowly escaped when the bus was set on fire. The second bus managed to avoid the mob and headed directly for Birmingham. However, in the terminal as the activists tried to leave the bus, the group was attacked by another white mob wielding lead pipes, baseball bats, and large chains.

The vicious assaults shocked the nation, but Alabama government and law enforcement officials refused to guarantee protection for Freedom Riders or prosecute their assailants. Robert F. Kennedy, who had been named Attorney General by his brother, sent an assistant, John Seigenthaler, to meet with Alabama governor John Patterson, who refused to help. While those who had been attacked left Birmingham and flew to New Orleans, SNCC members arrived from Nashville and promised to continue the journey. On May 20, twenty-seven Freedom Riders set off from Birmingham for Montgomery, but when they arrived, there was no one in sight at the bus terminal. Suddenly, as they alighted from the bus, hundreds of armed whites appeared with pipes and clubs and began beating the Freedom Riders. Although news cameramen were able to capture the assaults on film, the police were nowhere to be found.

King contacted Ralph Abernathy in Montgomery and said he was coming to Montgomery to take a stand with the SNCC students. When Robert Kennedy learned of this, he called King and told him that he could not guarantee his safety. But King made it clear he had to go. When Kennedy learned that Governor Patterson refused to call up the National Guard to protect the Freedom Riders, Kennedy, as Attorney General, ordered five hundred federal marshals to assemble at nearby Maxwell Air Force Base. King and Wyatt T. Walker arrived in Montgomery on Saturday. That evening a mass meeting was to be held at Abernathy's First African Baptist Church in support of the Freedom Riders.

Several hundred people gathered at First African in downtown Montgomery, but outside hundreds of whites began to surround the building. When Rev. Fred Shuttlesworth pushed his way through the crowd with CORE leader James Farmer and entered the church, the crowd exploded, throwing rocks and bricks at the church windows, overturning cars and setting them ablaze as others hurled tear gas bombs through broken windows. King went down to the church basement and called Robert Kennedy and told him what was happening. Kennedy assured King that the federal marshals were on their way. King went to the church door, and saw that the marshals had arrived and were trying to break up the mobs. But when he opened the doors to look out, he was showered with rocks, glass, and a tear gas bomb that just missed his head.

Those trapped in the church began praying and singing, but no one panicked. King went to the pulpit and explained what was happening outside and reassured them of their safety. About midnight the commotion outside the church died down, and King went out and spoke with General Henry V. Graham, who commanded a unit of National Guardsmen. General Graham said that although the guardsmen were beginning to disperse the crowd, it would be better if those persons in the church remained there all night. At about 5:00 the next morning, the Guardsmen began escorting the protesters out of the church to their homes. What came to be known as "The Battle of Montgomery" had ended.

That day the student-led Freedom Riders informed King that they were going to continue their journey and they wanted him to join them. But King was advised not to participate because he was still on probation in Georgia. If he was arrested again, he would have to go to jail and stay. The students were very disappointed with King's decision, and some later claimed that King lost a great deal of respect in their eyes when he did not join them. But King felt he had little choice. As the Freedom Riders left Montgomery, they were escorted by National Guardsmen to the state line. When they arrived in Jackson, Mississippi, they all were arrested. Throughout the summer of

1961, Freedom Riders continued to descend on Jackson, and were all arrested. Many were released from jail only after the bond was paid, payment made possible through the fund-raising activities of King and SCLC.

In the long run, however, the Freedom Riders were successful in bringing about an end to Jim Crow segregation in interstate bus transportation. In August 1961, the Interstate Commerce Commission (ICC) began holding hearings on the practices of bus companies operating in the South and issued a ban on racial segregation and discrimination in interstate transportation which took effect in November 1961.

In June 1961, when King, CORE's James Farmer, and several SNCC students met with Attorney General Kennedy, Kennedy encouraged these leaders to spur their groups to increase the number of southern black voters: This was one sure route to political power. While King had long supported voter registration projects, Kennedy's suggestion led to a split within SNCC between those who supported voter registration and others who wanted to continue the direct-action protests and confrontations. The issue came to a head at the SNCC annual meeting held at the Highlander Folk School in August 1961. The two camps reached a compromise and SNCC was divided into sections or wings, one-headed by Diane Nash, that would concentrate on direct-action protests, and the other, dealing with voter registration, to be headed by Charles Jones. The new SNCC chairman, James Forman, worked with both groups. He was also able to strengthen SNCC's organizational structure and raise funds for its activities. However, both SNCC and SCLC activists soon discovered that the fine distinctions that they were drawing between "direct-action protests" and "voter registration" had little meaning to white political leaders who vowed to crush, one way or another, any attempt by black or white civil rights activists to change the racial status quo in the South. This reality was made depressingly clear in the failed civil rights campaign in Albany, Georgia, in 1961 and 1962.

Albany, Georgia, was a small city of 60,000 located in the southwestern part of the state. Although African Americans made up more than 40 percent of the population, only a few blacks were registered to vote, and none held political office or served on the local police force. Jim Crow segregation was rigidly enforced in public places throughout the city, and although there was a local NAACP branch, it was not involved in civil rights activities. In May 1961, a NAACP Youth Council was organized, however, drawing members from the local public schools and the all-black Albany State College. When SNCC activists Charles Sherrod and Cordell Reagon arrived in Albany in October 1961, the Youth Council members were ready to act, with or without the approval of the parent branch.

On November 1, 1961, Sherrod, Reagon, and seven others, including Youth Council members, staged a sit-in at the Albany bus terminal to test the new ICC ban on racial segregation. When threatened with arrest, the students left, but later filed complaints against local bus officials for ignoring the ICC ruling. Following the protest, a mass meeting was held on November 17, 1961, where the representatives of ministerial alliances, the NAACP, the Federation of Women's Clubs, the Negro Voter League, and several other groups formed the Albany Movement, and Dr. William Anderson, a prominent physician, was chosen president. After five students were arrested by Albany's sheriff, Laurie Pritchett, during a demonstration at the Trailways Bus Terminal, the Albany Movement held its first mass meeting on November 25, and plans were made for a mass rally at City Hall to protest the students' arrests and trial.

More SNCC workers arrived in Albany early in December and organized several demonstrations. These demonstrations took place at the Albany train station, and scores were arrested. A few days later, at City Hall during the trial of those arrested at the train station, over two hundred more high school and college students were arrested. A march on City Hall and a "prayer vigil" were held on Wednesday, December 13, and another two hundred protesters were arrested. Most refused to be released on bail. Sheriff Pritchett made it clear that, in his words, "We can't tolerate the NAACP or SNCC or any other nigger organization to take over this town with mass demonstrations." Georgia governor Ernest Vandiver decided to send 150 National Guardsmen to Albany to augment the local police force.

Albany Movement president Dr. William Anderson invited King to address the mass meeting scheduled for Friday, December 15. While many welcomed King's presence and participation in the demonstrations, the SNCC organizers objected vehemently. They believed that the local leadership

King confronts Albany, Georgia, sheriff Laurie Pritchett.

could sustain the movement's momentum. When King arrived, Albany's Shiloh Baptist Church was filled with over 1,000 people and the music of protest.

As the people sang and shouted, King told them that "before the victory is won some must face physical death to free their children from a life of psychological handicaps. But we shall overcome." The audience responded with shouts of "Yes, Lord, we shall overcome." "Don't stop now," King shouted. "Keep moving! Walk together children. Don't get weary. There's a great camp meeting coming!"

King agreed to lead a march on City Hall the next day if city officials refused to release the demonstrators and failed to act on the black community's demands. The next morning, December 16, the Albany Movement leaders went to City Hall, but Mayor Asa Kelley refused to negotiate with them. King returned to Shiloh Baptist that afternoon to lead the march. With Dr. Anderson and Ralph Abernathy at his side, King led over three hundred demonstrators out of the church and into the street and then headed for the bus station. There, for the first time, King stood face-to-face with Sheriff Pritchett and his deputies. Pritchett told them they had no parade permit and would be arrested. King and the others knelt down and prayed; Pritchett and his men loaded hundreds of demonstrators into the waiting paddy wagons.

At the city jail King was charged with several misdemeanors, but refused to pay the bond. "I will refuse to pay the fine" he told the jailer. "I expect to spend Christmas in jail. I hope thousands will join me." While King, Abernathy, and Anderson were in jail, SNCC organizer Charles Jones left jail on bond, and convinced several Albany Movement leaders to make a deal with city officials. After announcing to the press that they did not need outside assistance, Albany Movement

ALBANY'S SINGING MOVEMENT

Growing up in Albany, I learned that if you bring black people together, you bring them together with a song." Bernice Johnson (Reagon) was a student at all-black Albany State College in 1961 and a member of the Youth Chapter of the local NAACP. Her father was a minister and she was used to singing a cappella at the church services. When SNCC organizers Charles Sherrod and Cordell Reagon arrived in the city and began organizing civil rights demonstrations, Bernice Johnson was arrested in the second wave of protests. When she arrived at the jail, her friend Slater King was already there. "Bernice, is that you?" King asked and Johnson responded "Yeah." "Sing a song."

Freedom songs became an important part of civil rights marches and demonstrations. The songs were used to generate a spirit of camaraderie among the protesters and became as widely known as the demonstrations themselves. Bernice Johnson recalled in an interview for the television documentary "Eyes on the Prize" that while singing "Over My Head I See Trouble in the Air" at a mass meeting at Union Baptist Church in Albany, "by the time I got to where 'trouble' was supposed to be, I didn't see any trouble so I put 'freedom' in there–'Up Above My Head, I See Freedom in the Air.'" The words of the spirituals were also changed to fit the new freedom struggle. "This Little Light of Mine, I'm Going to Let It Shine," which Johnson had been singing all her life, took on new meaning. "All in the street, I'm going to let it shine; All in the jailhouse, I'm going to let it shine, let it shine, let it shine, let it shine."

By 1962 the spiritual "We Shall Overcome" had been sung at hundreds of demonstrations organized by SCLC and SNCC, with the words of the chorus changed to fit each occasion and challenge faced by the protesters. In 1962, Bernice Johnson, Charles Nehlett, Rutha Mae Harris, and Cordell Reagon became the original members of the Freedom Singers, sponsored by SNCC. The group traveled around the country performing freedom songs and raising funds for the movement.

and SNCC leaders entered into an agreement with city officials. The agreement called for a cessation of demonstrations for thirty days in return for the release of the jailed protesters and city compliance with the ICC directive calling for desegregation of bus and train terminals. A biracial committee was to be appointed to work on other demands.

Upon hearing of the agreement, King allowed local leaders to pay his bond and shortly afterward left the city believing that the Albany Movement had achieved its objectives. But that was not the case. City officials were well aware of the divisions within the Albany Movement, and exploited them to bring about the end to the demonstrations. The officials had no intention of moving on black demands for the desegregation of parks, restaurants, theaters, and other public places in Albany. King later said he was sorry he let them bail him out.

Sporadic demonstrations and a boycott of downtown merchants and city buses began again in Albany when it became clear that city officials were not living up to the agreement, but soon the local bus company closed down altogether. King returned to Atlanta and began working with his staff on recruiting volunteers for the SCLC "Freedom Corps." King then made a "People-to-People" speaking tour of the Mississippi Delta area for the voter registration and direct-action projects. King also began publishing a biweekly column in the New York *Amsterdam News*. The column was similar to King's monthly column, "Advice for Living," that appeared in *Ebony* magazine between October 1957 and September 1958.

On February 27, 1962, King and Abernathy returned to Albany for their trial. After hearing testimony for only two hours, Judge A. N. Durden recessed the proceedings and said he would render a verdict in sixty days. There were only sporadic protests organized by the Albany Movement over the next few months.

Andrew Young, who had joined SCLC in 1961 to head the Citizenship School Program, recalled that he, Dorothy Cotton, and James Bevel organized workshops for the students and young people during the early months of 1962. Young recalled that in these workshops "we discovered an uncut diamond among the Albany students in sixteen-year-old Bernice Johnson." During the first session she and several others began singing, "and it seemed as if all the kids could sing, but Bernice's voice was as rich as the soil around Albany, with the texture of all the suffering of black folk that made the crops grow. Their singing brought a special spirit to the movement." Singing became such an important element in Albany that the campaigns there were often referred to as "The Singing Movement."

In Albany, the largest demonstration in the spring of 1962 was a march on City Hall in April following the shooting of a black man by the police. Twenty-nine people, including King and Abernathy, were arrested at that time. When King and Abernathy returned on July 10, 1962, the judge fined them $178; if they failed to pay, they were to serve a forty-five-day sentence in jail. Both refused to pay the fine and were sent to jail. Their sentence and incarceration reinvigorated the Albany Movement, and a mass rally and march on City Hall was held afterward at which thirty-two persons were arrested. Later that evening there were violent clashes in the city between police and black youths. On July 13, because of the increasing racial tensions, Sheriff Pritchett decided to release King and Abernathy from jail, claiming that "an unidentified Negro man" had paid their fines. When they asked who this man was, Sheriff Pritchett refused to answer. According to one account, Abernathy remarked, "I've been thrown out of lots of places in my day, but never before have been thrown out of jail!"

Demonstrations continued in Albany, however, and the governor, Ernest Vandiver, again sent National Guardsmen to bolster the local police. During another "prayer pilgrimage" to City Hall a few days later, King, Abernathy, and Dr. Anderson were arrested again, and they joined hundreds already jailed. Wave after wave of demonstrators held nonviolent protests at lunch counters, movie theaters, and parks throughout the city, and the police came and nonviolently placed them in paddy wagons and took them away to jail. Violence did erupt on the streets of Albany on July 24, when the pregnant wife of a protest leader was knocked unconscious by a policeman after she had visited her husband in jail. She later suffered a miscarriage. Despite a statement by President Kennedy on August 1 calling on blacks and whites in Albany to begin negotiations to end the demonstrations, Sheriff Pritchett kept filling up all the jails throughout the entire area with protesters. Coretta came to Albany to visit her husband in jail and brought all their children with her, including Dexter, the youngest child, named for Dexter Avenue Baptist Church, who at the time was only a year and a half old. Yolanda wanted her father to come home, but Coretta explained that he was in jail so that one day all people would be able to go wherever they liked. "Good," Yoki replied, "tell him to stay in jail until I can go to Funtown," a local amusement park.

On August 10, King and Abernathy were convicted again of parading without a permit, but they received a suspended sentence. Negotiations were scheduled between city officials and Albany Movement leaders, but King could not attend because he had to return to Atlanta. At the meeting on August 15, the commissioners adamantly refused to agree to any of the blacks' demands to desegregate public facilities in the city. Soon afterward officials closed all the public parks and sold the public swimming pools to a private corporation.

Meanwhile, all of Albany's public schools, restaurants, and movie theaters remained segregated. Thus after more than ten months of protests, demonstrations, sit-ins, and mass jailings, the Albany Movement had nothing to show for all of its efforts.

The failure to bring about desegregation in Albany provided important lessons for King and the other civil rights activists. They now realized that an entire black community could be mobilized to engage in nonviolent direct-action protests. The Albany Movement served as the model for organizations in other Georgia cities to carry out protest campaigns. Moreover, the confrontations in Albany demonstrated that careful organizing and planning by movement leaders were essential elements for the success of large mass demonstrations. All of the lessons learned in Albany were to be applied in the highly visible and often deadly confrontations with Sheriff Bull Connor and the Birmingham police force.

✦ ✦ ✦

"I have to make a faith act."

In 1956 and 1957, Rev. Fred Shuttlesworth and the Alabama Christian Movement for Human Rights (ACMHR) had taken the lead in campaigns to bring about the desegregation of Birmingham, the city that King called "the chief symbol of racial intolerance" in the South. With the formation of SCLC in 1957, ACMHR became its local affiliate, and Rev. Shuttlesworth continued as the courageous leader of the civil rights protests in Birmingham, where all public accommodations remained rigidly segregated. Rev. Shuttlesworth's home was bombed on Christmas night, 1956, because of his efforts to desegregate the local public transportation system. When he tried to enroll his children in an all-white public school in September 1957, he was attacked and beaten by a group of whites. In June 1958, Shuttlesworth sent a letter to Birmingham mayor James Morgan complaining about police brutality and harassment of black citizens, and a few days later his church, Bethel Baptist, was dynamited.

King and the SCLC leaders decided in September 1962 to begin demonstrations in Birmingham, including calling for a Christmas season boycott of downtown merchants by the black community. On learning of SCLC plans, white moderates in Birmingham pushed through a referendum that replaced the city commission form of government with a "mayor-council charter," in the belief that the new structure would allow a more moderate mayor to control the excesses of the police, especially Sheriff Bull Connor. The referendum passed in November 1962 and called for the election of a new city government in March 1963, rather than in 1965. The Birmingham business community supported the referendum because they feared the effects of a black economic boycott. With the passage of the referendum and the possibility that moderate Albert Boutwell would become the new mayor, members of the chamber of commerce met with Rev. Shuttlesworth and urged him to call off the boycott. In return, the businessmen agreed to desegregate five department stores in the downtown area. Shuttlesworth agreed and called off the boycott. Sheriff Connor refused to recognize the agreement, however, and threatened to prosecute the store owners. The "colored" and "white" signs reappeared in the five stores, but it was too late to reestablish the boycott.

Connor's actions in the face of white businessmen's desire to desegregate their stores demonstrated to Martin Luther King, Jr., that direct-action protests were the only effective means of achieving social change in Birmingham. In January 1963, SCLC held a two-day meeting in Dorchester, Georgia, and rescheduled protests and demonstrations to correspond with the Easter shopping season. SCLC executive director Wyatt T. Walker later recalled that "we decided on Birmingham with the attitude that we may not win, we may lose everything. But we knew that as Birmingham went, so would go the South."

For King, however, the most important objective was to expose the racial conditions in Birmingham in order to force the federal government to take a firm stand against continued racial discrimination. "The key to everything is federal commitment," King stated in a later interview. "To cure injustices you must expose them before the light of human conscience and the bar of public opinion, regardless of whatever tensions that exposure generates."

In the early months of 1963, as King traveled around the country speaking and raising funds for the upcoming

At Birmingham's Sixteenth Street Baptist Church in 1963.

Birmingham campaign, he was also becoming increasingly concerned about FBI charges that two of his closest advisors, Stanley Levison and Jack O'Dell, were Communists. The FBI surveillance of Levison began in the late 1950s when he became an advisor to King and SCLC. By 1963 there were illegal wiretaps on Levison's phones. Justice Department officials warned King that they believed that Levison and O'Dell were Communists. King confronted his friends about the allegations and they told him of their past connections with Communist party officials, but assured him that they were not currently associated with the Communists. O'Dell and Levison wrote personal statements to King describing their earlier Communist connections and he was satisfied with their explanations. However, FBI director J. Edgar Hoover was not satisfied, and he kept the wiretaps on Levison's phones. By the end of 1963, the FBI had placed wiretaps on King's phones as well.

The demands of raising money and making preparations for the Birmingham campaign meant that King was spending less and less time at home, even as Coretta was pregnant with their fourth child. King tried to spend holidays at home and to be present for the children's birthdays, but his constant traveling was very difficult for him and his family. More and more, Coretta found herself making decisions about important family matters alone. King was in New York City meeting with entertainer Harry Belafonte to establish a committee that would raise funds to pay bail bonds for protesters in Birmingham when he learned that Coretta was close to delivery. He rushed back to Atlanta and was at the hospital on March 28, 1963, when their fourth child was born. They named her Bernice Albertine, and called her Bunny.

In Birmingham, the mayoral election on March 5, 1963, had produced no winner. There was to be a runoff election on

April 2 between Albert Boutwell and Sheriff Bull Connor. This forced SCLC organizers to change their timetable for what they were calling Project "C." In the run-off election, Boutwell defeated Connor by over 8,000 votes and although he was considered moderate on racial issues, some SCLC staff thought of him as "just a dignified Bull Connor." However, several black leaders suggested that SCLC postpone its demonstrations in order to give the new city administration time to respond to their demands. Having learned from his Albany experience, King set out to unify the local black leaders. "I spoke to 125 business and professional people at a meeting in the Gaston Building. I talked to a gathering of two hundred ministers. I met with many small groups, during a hectic one-week schedule. In most cases, the atmosphere when I entered was tense and chilly, and I was aware that there was a great deal of work to be done."

After the runoff election, Bull Connor and the others who lost challenged the election's results. They refused to relinquish their offices, claiming that under the old government, their terms of office did not expire until November 1965. This meant that until the courts ruled on the issue, Connor would remain in control of the Birmingham police. On "B" Day, Wednesday, April 3, 1963, King issued the "Birmingham Manifesto," which called for the desegregation of all lunch counters, department stores, rest rooms, and drinking fountains in downtown department and variety stores, the hiring of black workers in business and industry, and the formation of a biracial committee to develop a schedule for the desegregation of all other areas of public life. Project "C" began that day when sixty-five protesters staged a sit-in at five downtown department stores. Twenty protesters were immediately dragged away by the police. Over the next three days other protesters were arrested on trespassing charges, and mass meetings were held nightly in black churches throughout the city.

The following week, small groups of protesters were parading downtown to City Hall and picketing in front of department stores. Connor was arresting hundreds as they marched, but the SCLC staff was posting their bail as soon as they were arrested and they returned immediately to the picket lines. On April 10, Connor served King, Abernathy, Andrew Young, and other SCLC leaders with a state court injunction prohibiting further demonstrations. The injunction had become a favorite weapon for state officials to prevent civil rights protests, but this time King decided that on Good Friday, April 12, 1963, he would violate the injunction and stage a march on City Hall. However, on Thursday, April 11, King was informed that SCLC had run out of bail money for those already jailed, and that no additional funds were forthcoming. What was King to do? He had promised those who marched that SCLC would provide bail money. King later recalled that "I sat in the deepest quiet I have ever felt, with two dozen others in the room." He walked into another room in the hotel suite where they were meeting, and was alone. "I thought of the 20 million black people who dreamed that someday they might be able to cross the Red Sea of injustice and find their way to the promised land of integration and freedom. There was no more room for doubt." King changed into work clothes and went back into the room with the others and declared, "I don't know what will happen; I don't know where the money will come from. But I have to make a faith act."

King led a group to Zion Hill Baptist Church where the people were waiting. He strode to the pulpit and told them he was heading for the Birmingham jail. King led a group of fifty downtown and right up to the police barricades where Bull

Connor was waiting for them, shouting. King and Abernathy knelt, said a prayer. At that point the police grabbed them by their belts and pushed them and all the marchers into paddy wagons. King had been arrested for the thirteenth time.

King was thrown into solitary confinement and was allowed no visitors. He was despondent. On Easter Sunday, however, the jailers allowed two of his attorneys to see him. That Monday, Clarence Jones, a New York attorney, came and told him that Harry Belafonte had raised $50,000 for bail money, and would find whatever funds King needed. He was also allowed to phone Coretta. She told him she had been very worried and called the Kennedys. President Kennedy had just spoken to her. Attorney General Robert Kennedy talked with Birmingham authorities in an effort to get King released from solitary confinement. But on Tuesday, April 16, King's attorney brought him a copy of the *Birmingham News*, which carried two statements about the demonstrations. One was signed by black clergymen and praised King and the marchers and called for immediate negotiations with city officials. The other statement was signed by eight Protestant and Jewish clergymen who condemned the demonstrations, branded King and SCLC "outside agitators," praised the local police for their "restraint," and called on blacks in Birmingham to avoid overt protests and to use the courts to settle their grievances.

As King read the latter statement, he decided to write an "open letter" responding to the white clergymen's charges. Written on scraps of paper given to him by a prison trustee and smuggled out by his attorneys, King composed his famous "Letter from a Birmingham Jail," which served as his major statement vindicating the nonviolent direct-action protest movement. In the letter, King responded to the clergymen's suggestion that King and SCLC were "outside agitators" by pointing out that they were in Birmingham because "injustice is here." And to those who argued that the demonstrations in Birmingham were "untimely," King said that he had never participated in a nonviolent direct-action protest that the oppressor thought was "well-timed."

The letter ended with King's expression of his extreme disappointment in the southern white churches and their response to segregation in general and the civil rights movement in particular. To a very great extent, the churches upheld the status quo. "I have watched white churchmen stand on the sideline and mouth pious irrelevancies and sanctimonious trivialities." But with the contemporary struggle for equal rights, the church risked becoming irrelevant if it did not return to its earlier spirit of sacrifice and commitment to justice.

The letter was smuggled out of the jail one page at a time, and typed by Wyatt T. Walker and others in the Gaston Motel. It was subsequently published in *Christian Century*, *Liberation*, and several other periodicals. The first pamphlet version was published by the American Friends Service and sold to raise money for the civil rights campaigns. Most scholars and historians believe King's "Letter from a Birmingham Jail" is a classic work in the black protest tradition in the United States and one of the finest statements of the philosophy and objectives of nonviolent protest ever written.

King and Abernathy left jail on April 20, and each day of the following week King, Abernathy, Walker, and Shuttlesworth were in court charged with "civil contempt," but the judge reduced the charge to a lesser crime and gave them five days in jail beginning May 16. Meanwhile, the demonstrations had slowed to almost nothing, primarily because most of the Birmingham adults willing to go to jail had already been arrested.

However, James Bevel, Dorothy Cotton, and Bernard Lee—King's younger associates—had been trying to recruit volunteers from the black colleges and high schools. Children and young adults turned out in droves to attend SCLC workshops on nonviolence, but King was at first reluctant to send children out into the streets to face Bull Connor's police. Finally, King agreed to do it because the nation needed to see schoolchildren marching for freedom. "I hope to subpoena the conscience of the nation to the judgment seat of morality."

On May 2, 1963, over 1,000 students showed up at Sixteenth Street Baptist Church and the so-called D-Day demonstrations began under the leadership of James Bevel. The students marched on the downtown area. As soon as they were met by Bull Connor's police, they were loaded into paddy wagons. Wave after wave of students marched into the downtown area and by nightfall more than nine hundred had been arrested. The next day, thousands of students again assembled at Sixteenth Street Baptist Church, but this time, as they attempted to leave the building and headed for Kelly Ingram Park, they were attacked by police dogs, and officers turned water hoses on them. Some ran in fear, trying to escape the water. Photographers and cameramen captured the vicious and unrelenting attacks on film and within days the images had been transmitted around the world. When President Kennedy viewed the police outrages on television, he said it made him "sick." The president sent Burke Marshall, head of the Civil Rights Division of the Justice Department, to Birmingham to meet with local officials to try and bring a halt to the police violence.

On Saturday, May 4, the marchers continued their protests and the police again attacked, but by Sunday, May 5, even the police were beginning to feel intimidated by the strength and persistence of the demonstrators. When a group of several hundred children and adults marched from New Pilgrim Baptist Church to hold a prayer meeting for those in jail, Sheriff Connor shouted, "Dammit. Turn on the hoses!," but his men froze. "Bull Connor's men, their deadly hoses poised for action, stood facing the marchers," King observed. "The marchers, many of them on their knees, stared back, unafraid and unmoving. Slowly the Negroes stood up and began to advance. Connor's men, as though hypnotized, fell back, their hoses sagging uselessly in their hands while several hundred Negroes marched past them, without further interference, and held a prayer meeting as planned."

Burke Marshall arrived in Birmingham and began meeting with white business leaders who were anxious to come to some agreement. The ongoing economic boycott of downtown stores had already wreaked havoc on their finances. The daily demonstrations kept white customers from the downtown area as well. While the jails were completely filled by Tuesday, May 7, downtown shopping had come to a complete halt. That afternoon, while Sheriff Connor's men again attacked the protesters with water hoses, the leading white businessmen decided that they wanted to reach some kind of settlement. That evening they agreed to desegregate the lunch counters, rest rooms, fitting rooms, and drinking fountains in their stores within a specific period of time; blacks would be employed on a nondiscriminatory basis in all Birmingham industries; protesters who had been jailed would be released without posting bond; and a biracial committee would be formed to maintain lines of communication between the black and white communities.

While Albert Boutwell sent representatives to the negotiations, Bull Connor realized what was happening and asked Governor George Wallace to send in the state police. By the evening of May 7, 575 state troopers under the direction of State Public Safety Director Albert Lingo were in Birmingham, and in an attempt to destroy the agreement, Connor had King and Abernathy arrested on an earlier charge. Although the bail for each man was set at $2,500, it was paid immediately by black businessman A. G. Gaston. King and Abernathy announced that they were suspending the demonstrations for twenty-four hours during the negotiations. Finally, on Friday, May 10, both groups emerged from the meeting and announced that an accord had been reached.

Martin Luther King, Jr. had every reason to be proud of the agreement. Within ninety days the downtown lunch counters, fitting rooms, and drinking fountains were desegregated; blacks began to be hired as clerks and salespersons in department stores; and the protesters were released.

The agreement had highly vocal critics from both sides. Rev. Shuttlesworth was in the hospital when the agreement was announced, and when he learned about King's plan to call off demonstrations, Shuttlesworth vowed to continue them, shouting at King, "You go to a point and then you stop. You won't be stopping here!" Andrew Young, who had worked hard to obtain the accord, recalled that it was only a telephone call from Attorney General Robert Kennedy, assuring Rev. Shuttlesworth of the validity of the agreement, that "satisfied his principles, soothed his wounded ego, and saved me from punching him out." When white politicians began to denounce those city officials who allowed themselves to be "whipped by the Negroes," mayor-elect Albert Boutwell disavowed any responsibility for the agreement.

King left Birmingham for Atlanta on Saturday, May 11, to be with his family for Mother's Day. At home late that night he received a desperate call from his brother, A. D. King, in Birmingham. A.D.'s home had been bombed along with the Gaston Motel, where several persons were injured. In retaliation, blacks in Birmingham had begun rioting. Two stores and a taxi were set on fire, and a policeman was stabbed before Lingo's state troopers began attacking and beating blacks on the streets with gun butts and billy clubs. A. D. King and other black ministers were out in the streets trying to disperse the crowds. King returned to Birmingham the next day and was on the streets with the other ministers trying to prevent further rioting. President Kennedy federalized the Alabama National Guard and placed 3,000 federal troops in military installations nearby.

The U.S. Supreme Court ruled on May 23 that the newly elected Boutwell city government was legal, and therefore Bull Connor and his city commissioners were no longer in office. Despite the rioting, the agreement King worked out with the Birmingham businessmen held, and the new city government soon rescinded Birminham's segregation ordinances.

The police brutality, bombings, and rioting in Birmingham; Governor George Wallace "standing in the schoolhouse door" symbolically blocking the registration of two black students at the University of Alabama in June 1963; and the other civil rights issues deeply disturbed President Kennedy, who felt it was time to assert his leadership before events escalated beyond his control. He decided to go on television to announce that he was sending to Congress a Civil Rights Bill that would make the kinds of discrimination in public accommodations that King had struggled against in Birmingham subject to federal law.

Virtually all of President Kennedy's Cabinet members opposed the legislation's introduction. Attorney General Robert Kennedy alone supported the decision. The brothers both understood that this was a moral issue. "It is as old as the

Scriptures and as dear as the American Constitution," President Kennedy declared in his televised address to the nation. "The heart of the question is whether all Americans are to be afforded equal rights and equal opportunities; whether we are going to treat our fellow Americans as we want to be treated." That same night, June 11, 1963, Medgar Evers, the NAACP field secretary, was gunned down in front of his home in Jackson, Mississippi, by a white man. Charles Evers, Medgar's brother, recalled that "Bobby [Kennedy] sat with me during the funeral, and he consoled me. President Kennedy carried Mrs. Evers and I and the children back to the White House. We stayed there for the rest of the day." When the Civil Rights Bill was sent to Congress on June 19, Robert Kennedy took charge and began to organize support for the legislation in the business, labor, religious, and educational communities.

Following the confrontations in Birmingham, Andrew Young later recalled that James Bevel, who had worked with the young people in Birmingham, came up with the idea that 8,000 people should march from Birmingham to Washington "in imitation of Gandhi's spectacular March to the Sea in India" to dramatize their dissatisfaction with the racial conditions in the South. While King supported the idea of a march, the task of supplying the physical needs of 8,000 people walking from Alabama to Washington, D.C., was too overwhelming to contemplate. However, Young pointed out that "the cross-country march never came off, but out of the germ of Bevel's idea came SCLC's commitment to the famous celebration of August 28, 1963."

circa 1964

CHAPTER FIVE

GOD LAID HIS HANDS ON ME

---◆---

The idea for the August 1963 March on Washington can be traced to A. Philip Randolph, president of the Brotherhood of Sleeping Car Porters. Randolph organized the March on Washington Movement in 1941, which had led to President Franklin D. Roosevelt's executive order creating the Fair Employment Practices Committee (FEPC). Randolph had also been instrumental in the Prayer Pilgrimage that took place at the Lincoln Memorial in Washington on May 17, 1957, in which Martin Luther King, Jr., emerged as a national civil rights leader. In the fall of 1962, Randolph suggested to a group of black labor leaders that an appropriate way to mark the centennial of the Emancipation Proclamation would be to organize a "massive Emancipation March on Washington" to draw national attention to one hundred years of "unfulfilled social and political promises." Randolph asked his close friend and associate Bayard Rustin to draw up a blueprint for such a march, which Rustin submitted in January 1963. Rustin's plan called for "the coordinated participation of all progressive sectors of the liberal, labor, religious, and Negro communities."

Rustin had been one of the founders of SCLC, but he had been asked to sever his relationship with the organization by King in 1960 after Congressman Adam Clayton Powell threatened to make public his accusation that there was a sexual relationship between King and Rustin. There was no truth to this charge, but Powell wanted King and A. Philip Randolph to cancel the proposed protests at the Democratic National Convention in Los Angeles. Despite Powell's objections, the protests took place, but Rustin's association with SCLC ended. Novelist and civil rights advocate James Baldwin, in an article in *Harper's* magazine in February 1961, commented that to sever Rustin's connection to SCLC "on the basis of a completely false accusation meant that King lost much moral credit . . . in the eyes of the young."

When Rustin submitted his plan for the Emancipation March to Randolph in January 1963, King was immersed in preparations for the Birmingham demonstrations. Randolph asked King to consider the project, but at first King demurred because he was still contemplating the possibility of a SCLC-sponsored march. When Randolph made it clear to King that the proposed demonstration would be for civil rights and economic advancement, King came on board.

The momentum for the march was built up by the televised reports of the demonstrations in Birmingham which had spurred President Kennedy to introduce his Civil Rights Bill to Congress. However, when John and Robert Kennedy received the news about the proposed march on Washington, they were dismayed and decided to convene a conference in the Cabinet Room at the White House with the "Big Six" black leaders: King, Wilkins, Randolph, Farmer, SNCC's John Lewis, and Whitney Young of the National Urban League. Arthur Schlesinger, Jr., a presidential advisor, attended the meeting, along with the Kennedys and Lyndon B. Johnson. He recalled that the president voiced his concerns about the march's impact on the prospects for passage of the Civil Rights Bill. King defended the march and reiterated the point that he had never engaged in a direct-action protest that was considered well timed.

As the meeting was breaking up, President Kennedy took King aside and they walked together in the Rose Garden. King

The "Big Six" with President Kennedy. Front, from left: Whitney Young, John Lewis, King, Rabbi Joachim Prinz, A. Philip Randolph, Kennedy, Walter Reuther, and Roy Wilkins.

later told Andrew Young that the president voiced his concern about FBI reports that Stanley Levison and Jack O'Dell were Communists. King asked if the president had seen the evidence for these allegations himself. Although Kennedy said he had not seen the FBI's evidence, he told King, "You've got to get rid of them." Kennedy believed that if the opponents of the Civil Rights Bill "shoot you down, they'll shoot us down too— so we're asking you to be careful."

Afterward King met with Jack O'Dell, who said he knew his phones were tapped and he was under surveillance. O'Dell offered his resignation from SCLC. Later, Stanley Levison talked with King about the president's entreaties, and they both agreed to end contact because Levison also knew he was under FBI surveillance and he too did not want to jeopardize the success of the Civil Rights Bill. King informed Attorney General Kennedy of O'Dell and Levison's decisions, and at a press conference on July 17, 1963, President Kennedy stated that there was "no evidence" of Communist influence on the civil rights movement.

Although there were objections raised by the NAACP's Roy Wilkins at a meeting of the civil rights leaders on July 2, 1963, they agreed to make A. Philip Randolph the official director of the March on Washington planned for August 28, 1963, and chose Bayard Rustin as the "chief organizer." Rustin's objective was to mobilize up to 100,000 demonstrators to participate in a nonviolent protest at the nation's capitol. The Big Six also voted to add four white co-chairmen of the march: Walter Reuther of the United Auto Workers Union, Rabbi Joachim Prinz of the American Jewish Congress, Rev. Eugene Carson Blake of the National Council of Protestant Churches, and Matthew Ahmann of the National Catholic Conference for Interracial Justice.

King traveled to Detroit, Los Angeles, Chicago, and Harlem, where he spoke to large crowds of people, participated in civil rights demonstrations, and spread the word about the upcoming March on Washington. Meanwhile, civil rights protests were organized in over 260 cities in the North and the South. Thousands of restaurants, stores, and public transportation systems were integrated, and blacks and whites marched in solidarity with those who were arrested for civil rights activities. In Danville, Virginia, King led a civil rights march in defiance of a court injunction.

On Tuesday, August 27, when King arrived in Washington, he had not finished the draft for the address he was to deliver. He continued to work on it in his room in the Willard Hotel, finally completing it in longhand after midnight when it was typed by his staff, copied, and later distributed to reporters.

King's speech was scheduled for the end of the program. Roy Wilkins and Whitney Young, who initially were reluctant to support the march, made sure that they had the prime positions on the march program. They assumed that the television reporters would leave after the opening speeches to prepare the spots for the evening news. As he worked on his speech in his hotel room, King began receiving reports that the number of participants was twice what they had projected, and at least 25 percent of those gathered were white. One sad note was reported at what otherwise was a joyful and triumphant event: The great African-American scholar and leader W.E.B. DuBois had died in exile in Accra, Ghana, at the age of ninety-five. More than any other leader, DuBois throughout his long and productive life laid the groundwork for the civil rights campaigns that culminated in the March on Washington.

Late in the afternoon, it came time for King to speak. He later recalled that "I started out reading the speech, just all of a sudden—the audience response was wonderful that day—and all of a sudden this thing came over me that I have used . . . and I just felt that I wanted to use it here. I don't know why I hadn't thought of it before the speech." Thus King dispensed with his prepared text, and spoke extemporaneously, beginning, "I have a dream that one day on the red hills of Georgia, the sons of former slaves and the sons of former slave-owners will be able to sit down together at the table of brotherhood." King's "I Have a Dream" speech became one of the most important and best-known speeches delivered in the twentieth century and served as an inspiration to oppressed peoples in the United States and throughout the world. With this speech Martin Luther King, Jr., emerged as the most prominent black leader in the United States.

President Kennedy met with the march leaders at a reception in the White House at the end of the day, and congratulated them on their great success. Members of Congress, though,

The March on Washington, 1963.

appeared to be untouched and there was no movement on the Civil Rights Bill. And in Birmingham, racists planted a bomb in the Sixteenth Street Baptist Church. It exploded on Sunday morning, September 15, 1963, and killed four young girls—Denise McNair, Carole Robertson, Cynthia Wesley, and Addie Mae Collins, who were preparing for Sunday school—and injured many others. For many young civil rights activists this was another incident that served to undermine their commitment to "nonviolence." Protest rallies were organized throughout the country. King delivered the eulogy at the funeral for three of the girls and managed to hold in check the bitterness he felt toward the local white community and its leadership, which did not even bother to respond in outrage to these and other murders that had occurred in the city. King declared, "The innocent blood of these little girls may well serve as the redemptive force that will bring new light to this dark city."

There were other negative responses to the March on Washington in general, and to King's rise as the preeminent black leader. Malcolm X, who had gained an international reputation while serving as the main spokesman for Elijah Muhammad's Nation of Islam, a black separatist group, referred to the event as "the farce on Washington." While King advocated the integration of black people into American society on the basis of equality, Malcolm X gained national and international notoriety preaching black self-defense against unwarranted attacks by whites; in television and radio interviews, Malcolm labeled King and the other civil rights leaders "Uncle Toms" who had been paid by the "white devil" to keep the Negro "meek and servile." King saw himself and the civil rights movement he led as a viable alternative to the "extreme black nationalist ideologies" of Malcolm X and the Nation of Islam. In the "Letter from a Birmingham Jail," he had warned

Martin Luther King, Jr. and Malcolm X at their meeting, March 1964.

white liberals and conservatives that the "frustration and despair" in the black community could result in violence, "a development that will lead inevitably to a frightening racial nightmare." Eventually, Malcolm came to respect King and his philosophy.

King's success at the March on Washington also increased FBI director J. Edgar Hoover's growing hatred. The day after the march, William Sullivan, the FBI director of Domestic

Intelligence, sent Hoover a memo in which he declared that the Bureau must regard King "as the most dangerous Negro of the future in this Nation from the standpoint of Communism, the Negro, and National security." King regretted his earlier decision to break off all contact with his close advisor Stanley Levison because of FBI allegations that Levison was a Communist; and following the march, he began telephoning Levison for counsel and advice. Unfortunately, Levison's phone had been tapped by the FBI, and on October 7, 1963, Hoover joyfully informed Attorney General Robert Kennedy that King had broken his promise by contacting Levison. Fearful that renewed charges that King was a Communist would further damage the prospects for the Civil Rights Bill in Congress, Robert Kennedy reluctantly authorized wiretaps on King's home and offices. William Sullivan later reported that "Bobby Kennedy resisted, resisted, and resisted tapping King. . . . Finally we twisted the arm of the attorney general to the point where he had to go. I guess he feared we would let that stuff go in the press if he said no."

On November 22, 1963, King was at home in Atlanta preparing to leave on a fund-raising trip to Los Angeles. Suddenly a news bulletin came on the television: President Kennedy had been shot in Dallas, Texas, shortly after arriving for a political visit. Martin, Coretta, and King's assistant Bernard Lee gathered around the television and listened to the news reports, switching from channel to channel. Finally, at 2:30 P.M. the sad news was announced: John F. Kennedy was dead. Coretta King recalled that Martin listened intently to the reports. Finally, he said to her, "I don't think I'm going to live to reach forty." Coretta was disturbed by the statement, but he persisted, "This is what is going to happen to me also. I keep telling you, this is a sick nation. And I don't think I can survive either."

Lyndon Baines Johnson was now president of the United States. King had met Johnson on several occasions and believed he was sensitive to black needs and objectives. Unlike his fellow southerners, in the past Johnson had supported civil rights legislation. As Senate majority leader, Johnson was the major force behind the compromise that allowed the passage of the 1957 Civil Rights Act, and Johnson made it clear from the beginning of his presidency that he favored passage of the Civil Rights Bill. King met with President Johnson on December 3, 1963, to discuss legislative strategies, and afterward King declared that unless Johnson changed his course considerably, King would move forward believing in the president's commitment to civil rights.

Time magazine named King 1963's "Man of the Year" and his portrait appeared on the cover of the January 3, 1964, issue. This accolade was just another manifestation of the increasing recognition King was receiving for his eloquence, courage, and leadership. However, personally he was still very torn over his growing prominence, and often felt guilty about his success and recognition. "I'm no messiah," he repeated over and over again to those close to him, "and I don't have a messiah complex." While his extreme sensitivity to criticism could make him taciturn and depressed for days at a time, in private he also displayed a healthy sense of humor and was known to enjoy and even tell "preacher jokes." Most importantly, King wanted to be loved, and when he was on the road, away from his home for weeks at a time, he found it in the arms of women more than willing to provide the affection and physical outlet he so desperately needed. It was these liaisons that weighed heavily on King's conscience and kept him humble and very human in the eyes of those who were his intimates.

But what was most disturbing and causing the greatest self-doubt in early 1964 was the growing disillusionment, particularly among the young, with King's philosophy and practice of nonviolence. The novelist and social critic James Baldwin had begun predicting the violent response of younger blacks to their conditions and treatment in both the North and South from as early as 1961. In his book of autobiographical essays, *Nobody Knows My Name*, Baldwin predicted race violence in Atlanta, and "when a race riot occurs in Atlanta, it will not spread merely to Birmingham, for example (Birmingham is a doomed city). The trouble will spread to every metropolitan center in the nation which has a significant Negro population." In May 1964, Baldwin published *The Fire Next Time*, which remained at the top of the best-seller lists for the next six months. In that work, he concluded that one of the reasons for the growing influence of Elijah Muhammad, Malcolm X, and the Nation of Islam in black communities across the nation was their advocacy of "black self-defense" in the face of unprovoked attacks by whites. While Baldwin supported King and his commitment to nonviolence, he understood that given the anti-black prejudice and discrimination in these cities, anti-white violence was inevitable.

Early in 1964, King was contacted by Robert B. Hayling, a black dentist and Air Force veteran in St. Augustine, Florida. The black community there had been terrorized by the Klan for years and victimized regularly by police brutality, especially so in the last year, after Hayling organized a black voter-registration campaign in the summer of 1963. King was disturbed that federal authorities did not investigate and intervene in St. Augustine, which was about to celebrate its quadricentennial as America's Oldest City.

King sent C. T. Vivian, Hosea Williams, and Bernard Lee to St. Augustine to prepare the city's black residents for nonviolent struggle. In April 1964, the SCLC leaders began conducting night protest marches in St. Augustine's old "Slave Market." Andrew Young arrived just as one of the evening marches was about to begin. As he and a small group of protesters came within a block of the market, Young approached Hoss Mauncy, deputy sheriff and local Klan leader, and his gang to speak with them. Young was brutally attacked; he urged the marchers forward, and he was attacked again.

The white mob soon turned on the reporters with their cameras, clubbing several of them. Then Sheriff L. O. Davis suddenly appeared, probably realizing that the cameras had recorded enough brutality, and began to push the whites to the sidelines. The marchers continued to the market, knelt and prayed, and returned to the church without incident.

Given the violence, Young and the others tried to convince King to stay away from St. Augustine, since he was the prime target for Klan sharpshooters. But he went and led marches, was arrested, and served time in jail. At the end of May 1964, after a local court issued a ban on further civil rights demonstrations, SCLC went to federal court to seek protection for marchers. Federal District Judge Brian Simpson ruled on June 9, 1964, that the marches could continue, but Sheriff Davis merely shifted his tactics and arrested marchers as soon as they left the black churches. The demonstrations continued, and as St. Augustine's tourist season began, protesters held "swim-ins" at local beaches and hotel swimming pools.

The ongoing violence in St. Augustine stayed in the news as senators voted to end the filibuster launched by southern Democrats against the Civil Rights Bill. Florida governor C. Farris Bryant and attorney general James Kynes wanted to end the demonstrations in St. Augustine and finally announced

THE CIVIL RIGHTS ACT OF 1964

The Civil Rights Act of 1964 brought about the end of apartheid—legal racial segregation—in the United States.

The Act consists of ten titles. Title I prohibited the use of literacy tests as a qualification for voting in federal elections. Title II declared that all persons are entitled to "full and equal enjoyment of the goods, services, facilities, privileges, and advantages . . . of any place of public accommodation without discrimination or segregation . . ." In instances of discrimination, under Title III the U.S. attorney general—rather than the victim of the discrimination—was authorized to bring suit against offending individuals or agencies. Under the terms of Title IV, the attorney general was also authorized to bring suits to enforce public school desegregation.

Title V extended the life of the U. S. Commission on Civil Rights. One of the Act's most controversial provisions was Title VI, which directed all federal agencies to adopt regulations banning discrimination and called for the withholding of federal funds to any public or private agency that refused to comply.

Title VII prohibited employment discrimination by employers and labor unions with more than twenty-five members as well as employment agencies, and authorized the creation of the Equal Employment Opportunity Commission (EEOC), whose five members were to investigate complaints of employment discrimination, hold hearings, and make recommendations for action to the attorney general and to the Congress for future legislation.

Title VIII authorized the secretary of commerce to conduct a survey to determine the extent of voter registration and participation in state and national elections. Title IX authorized the attorney general to enter into any court cases dealing with discrimination, where the issues involved are deemed to be of "general public importance." And Title X established the Community Relations Service within the Department of Commerce to assist local communities "in resolving disputes, disagreements, or difficulties relating to discriminatory practices . . . wherever the peaceful relations among citizens of the community involved are threatened."

that they were appointing a biracial committee to negotiate civil rights demands. King and local leaders met with the state officials and it was clear that both groups wanted an end to the protests. The Civil Rights Bill had passed in the Senate and King was due in Washington on July 2 to attend the signing at the White House. The new law would address the specific practices SCLC had been protesting for months in St. Augustine, and the state officials promised to comply with its provisions. While it was extremely important and expanded the civil rights of the majority of Americans—not just African Americans—the law made no mention of discrimination in housing or the absence of voting rights for hundreds of thousands of black and Hispanic citizens in the southern and western states. The civil rights movement had come a long way, but there was still much unfinished business in July 1964.

Why We Can't Wait, King's latest book, was published during the St. Augustine demonstrations. It presented his personal perspective on the Birmingham campaign, and also pointed to new directions in his thought and activities. King discussed the economic insecurity and poverty of many blacks and whites in the United States, the wealthiest country on earth. He called for massive federal financial assistance to the poor, a "Bill of Rights for the Disadvantaged," similar to the GI Bill of Rights, that would raise standards of living and support educational advancement.

While SCLC was involved in St. Augustine, SNCC members organized Freedom Summer. This project brought several hundred northern black and white students to Mississippi to work in educational programs and voter-registration campaigns. King told his staff that Freedom Summer was the year's major civil rights initiative. John Lewis, Robert Moses, James Forman, and other SNCC leaders were interested in

King and Abernathy in the St. Augustine, Florida, jail, 1964.

bringing northern white students to Mississippi to engage in civil rights activities because they hoped that southern racists would be less willing to attack these young upperclass whites for fear of the negative consequences locally and nationally. However, the danger that lay ahead for all of these students was made dramatically clear early in the campaign when it was announced on June 21, 1964, that three young civil rights activists—James Chaney, Andrew Goodman, and Michael Schwerner—who had begun working in Mississippi had disappeared. A massive manhunt was set up—even J. Edgar Hoover came to the state to oversee FBI search operations. On August 4, the bodies of the three murdered men were finally discovered in an earthfill in Philadelphia, Mississippi.

The summer of 1964 also witnessed the first of the long series of urban riots that rocked the nation through the end of the decade. Rioting erupted in Harlem and Brooklyn, New York, on July 18, after a black teenager was killed by a white policeman. New York's Mayor Robert Wagner contacted King and asked him to come to the city to help quell the widespread violence. King went to New York City and met with black community leaders, who told him that "police brutality" was one major reason for the rioting. Later that summer, rioting also broke out in Rochester, New York; Paterson and Jersey City, New Jersey; and in Philadelphia, Pennsylvania. The increasing urban violence soon convinced King to take his civil rights campaigns to the North.

In August 1964, the entire nation witnessed the televised testimony of Fannie Lou Hamer, Aaron Henry, and the other members of the Mississippi Freedom Democratic Party (MFDP) before the Credentials Committee of the Democratic Convention in Atlantic City, in their ill-fated attempt to unseat the all-white delegation sent to represent the state. King also went to Atlantic City, testified before the Committee, and lobbied delegates to seat the black and white MFDP members at the convention. Unfortunately, President Johnson feared that seating the MFDP delegates would alienate southern white voters, and proposed a compromise in which the sixty-member delegation was offered two at-large seats. This was rejected. King supported the MFDP's decision, and told the delegates to return to Mississippi and work for the overthrow of the all-white Democratic political organization within the state.

In mid-September 1964, Martin, Coretta, and Ralph Abernathy traveled to West Berlin, Germany at the invitation of Mayor Willy Brandt. They also attended a memorial service for President Kennedy and King spoke at several churches. In Rome, King and Abernathy were given a private audience with Pope Paul VI, who promised to issue a statement condemning racial injustice. Afterward, the trio visited Madrid and London, where *Why We Can't Wait* had just been published. Upon returning to the United States at the end of the month, King and Abernathy prepared for the SCLC annual meeting to be held in Savannah, Georgia. The major issue on the agenda was getting out the black vote for the November 3 election, because King came to believe that the next phase of the civil rights struggle would involve political action. As SCLC's goals and objectives shifted from protesting segregation to black social and economic advancement, the focus became more national than southern. Political mobilization would be necessary to achieve this advancement.

After the SCLC annual meeting, King made trips to New York City, Newark, Philadelphia, and St. Louis and returned to Atlanta on Tuesday, October 12, completely exhausted. His doctor, Asa G. Yancey, found that King also had a severe virus infection and elevated blood pressure. Dr. Yancey decided to check King into St. Joseph's Infirmary. The next morning the Associated Press called King's home with the news that he had won the Nobel Peace Prize. Coretta was overcome with joy and called Martin immediately. King, still quite groggy, finally comprehended what she was saying. Within minutes the hospital waiting rooms filled with reporters, and after Coretta arrived, he held a brief press conference. King felt completely humbled by the award, offering praise to all those, black and white, who used nonviolent protests to advance the cause of civil rights. King later announced that most of the $54,600 prize money would be donated to SCLC, SNCC, CORE, the NAACP, the National Council of Negro Women, and the American Foundation for Peace.

King's spirits were buoyed by the news of the award, which helped speed his physical recovery. Within a week King was back on his feet. He traveled around the country speaking at "Get Out the Vote" rallies. In the November 3 elections, Lyndon Johnson won a landslide victory over Arizona Senator Barry Goldwater, who carried only six states. The Democrats increased their large majority over the Republicans in both houses of Congress.

As a result of the tremendous success of the March on Washington the previous year, Bayard Rustin was again working for SCLC. King also asked Rustin to coordinate his itinerary and activities for the trip to Norway to accept the Nobel Prize. Rustin arrived in England on November 12 and arranged for King to speak at a British anti-nuclear-arms rally, to meet with members of Parliament and other government officials, and to preach a sermon at St. Paul's Cathedral in London.

In the days and weeks following the announcement of the prize, King was inundated with cards, letters, and telegrams of congratulations from around the world. But not everyone was pleased about the award. The Nobel Prize Committee received numerous letters of protest about its choice and others publicly expressed their outrage. J. Edgar Hoover was incensed over the news (and envious, since he felt that he should have been awarded the Nobel Peace Prize). On November 18, 1964, at an interview with a group of newswomen, Hoover denounced King for his criticism of the FBI in the past and called him "the most notorious liar in the country." The statement made headlines in newspapers around the country and the world, and King, who was resting in Bimini at the time, was completely shocked. In a later public statement King suggested that Hoover must be working under some "extreme pressure" and that his mental state "has apparently faltered under the awesome burden, complexities and responsibilities of his office." Subsequently, CORE's James Farmer asked to meet with King. Farmer told King that Hoover was "determined to get him," and was spreading rumors that King had engaged in "group sex" in hotel rooms, had "Communist associations," and was guilty of "financial improprieties" related to SCLC. King vigorously denied the charges, and subsequently sent a telegram to Hoover asking for a face-to-face meeting. In the interim, Hoover authorized FBI assistant director Deke DeLoach to begin showing the dossier the FBI had compiled on King to various persons in the administration and Congress; they also tried to interest several newspaper journalists in it, but the journalists refused to print the salacious material.

Finally, a meeting took place in Hoover's office in Washington, D.C., on December 1, 1964. King was accompanied by Andrew Young, Ralph Abernathy, and Walter Fauntroy; Young recalled that Hoover was cordial, congratulated King on the Nobel Peace Prize, and tried to explain the FBI's problems operating in the South. "He was attempting to sell us on the virtues of the FBI, even in relation to civil rights." Hoover talked for about fifty minutes and gave King and his companions no opportunity to speak. There was no discussion of FBI surveillance, Communism, sex, or Hoover's statement that King was a "liar." Finally, as the meeting drew to a close, Ralph Abernathy thanked the director and said there were some things that they needed to discuss further and it would perhaps be better if King were not present. Hoover agreed and Young was assigned to make arrangements with Deke DeLoach for future meetings. The press was waiting outside and King summarized what took place. Young recalled that although the meeting had cleared the air somewhat, "it left us feeling vaguely dissatisfied because so much was left unsaid."

King was still disturbed and depressed over Hoover's statements as his family and a large group of friends gathered in New York City to help him prepare for the trip to Europe. King and his entourage left on December 4, 1964, and after spending four eventful days in London, arrived in Oslo, Norway, on December 8. On Thursday, December 10, King received the Peace Prize at a lavish ceremony at Oslo University in the presence of members of the Norwegian royal family and government officials. In his brief acceptance speech, he expressed his belief that the award demonstrated "a profound recognition that nonviolence is the answer to the crucial political and moral question of our time—the need for man to overcome oppression and violence without resorting to violence and oppression."

The Swedish Peace Council sponsored King's trip to Stockholm, where he preached in the national cathedral and at an evening rally celebrating the independence of the African nation of Kenya. When King and his entourage arrived back in the United States, fireboats saluted him in the East River in New York City, and over 10,000 people greeted him at the Harlem Armory. At a church service, King exclaimed how pleased he was with the award and recognition. "I really wish I could just stay on the mountain," he declared, "but I must go back to the valley." King stopped in Washington, D.C., on his way to Atlanta and met with President Johnson. King urged the president to give his full support to the voting rights bill then pending in Congress, but Johnson said he did not want to push new legislation so soon after the passage of the Civil Rights Act. Even as the two leaders met, however, SCLC officers had been laying the groundwork for protests against the denial of black voting rights in Selma, Alabama. If King had his way, there would be voting rights legislation passed by Congress in 1965, with or without the president's full support.

circa 1966

CHAPTER SIX

WE SHALL OVERCOME

---◆---

T he need for voting rights legislation was glaringly apparent in the Black Belt sections of Alabama, Mississippi, Louisiana, and other states in the deep South. In predominantly black Dallas, Perry, and Hale counties in Alabama, for example, less than 5 percent of the eligible black population was registered to vote. Similarly low registration figures existed in the predominantly black areas of Louisiana, Mississippi, and Georgia. SNCC organizers began to challenge these conditions in various parts of the South in 1962 and 1963. Bernard and Colia Lafayette targeted Dallas County, Alabama. In February 1963, with the assistance of local leaders Amelia Boynton and Frederick Reese, who had founded the Dallas County Voters League the year before, the Lafayettes began sponsoring a series of voter-registration drives. Unfortunately, the results were limited because the registration offices were open only two days each month, and those blacks who attempted to register were often rejected by the all-white board of registrars through the use of purposefully difficult and complex "literacy tests."

SNCC, the Dallas County Voters League, and the newly formed Dallas County Improvement Association persisted in their activities, sponsoring Freedom Day rallies in October 1963 and July 1964. Unfortunately, many blacks who participated in these activities, or who attempted to register to vote, were arrested by police for "parading without a permit" or "incitement to riot." The sheriff of Dallas County, James G. Clark, was known for his brutal treatment of blacks in general, and civil rights protesters in particular, and during the July 1964 rallies Sheriff Clark and his volunteer "posse" used tear gas and nightsticks on those attempting to register. Within days, state judge James J. Hare issued a sweeping injunction banning further voter-registration marches and rallies.

Sporadic demonstrations occurred in the fall of 1964, and following the local elections in November, Selma's new mayor, James T. Smitherman, appointed Wilson Baker, a former city police captain, director of public safety. Smitherman hoped that Baker would be able to prevent Sheriff Clark from using excessively brutal tactics against civil rights activists. Unfortunately, Baker proved less than effective in controlling Clark, and police abuse and brutality continued. In mid-November 1964, after a visit to Selma by SCLC's C. T. Vivian, Frederick Reese and the Dallas County Voters League invited SCLC to come to the city to assist in voter-registration campaigns. Some SNCC organizers already there were resentful of this decision, but they soon recognized the fund-raising and other benefits that resulted when King and his colleagues entered local civil rights campaigns.

King spoke at SCLC's first major rally in Selma, held at Brown Chapel on January 2, 1965. He told the more than five hundred people assembled that he was pursuing a "determined, organized, mobilized campaign to get the right to vote everywhere in Alabama." Another "Freedom Day" rally was scheduled for January 18, and SCLC staff member James Bevel remained in Selma to make preparations. Working with SNCC members John Lewis and Ivanhoe Donaldson, they arranged for most of Selma's black ministers to make their churches available for meetings and rallies. Volunteers were recruited from every section of the city to solicit individuals willing to participate in the voter-registration drive.

King returned to Atlanta, and two days later, on January 5, 1965, Coretta found and opened a box that had been delivered from SCLC headquarters. It contained a tape and a crudely written note addressed to King. Among other things the note accused King of being "a complete fraud and a great liability to all of us Negroes." The anonymous letter contained threats: "Your end is near. . . . You are finished. . . . King you are done" because you are "a dissolute, abnormal immoral imbecile." It suggested that King commit suicide: "There is only one thing left for you to do. You know what this is. You have just 34 days in which to do [it]." Coretta played the tape and found that it contained the sounds of people making love, and King's voice was on it. Coretta called her husband at his office. King, Abernathy, Andrew Young, and SCLC's lawyers concluded that this had to be the work of J. Edgar Hoover and the FBI. Needless to say, King was extremely disturbed by the recording because it furnished proof that his hotel rooms had been bugged. Coretta reiterated her loyalty to her husband, but they all agreed that the FBI must be confronted over the issue of buggings and wiretaps. When Abernathy and Young later met

King rallies the Selma marchers.

with FBI official Deke DeLoach, he of course denied any FBI knowledge of the package or tape, but the incident was clearly part of the campaign of "dirty tricks" against King. Although unnerved by this dreadful incident, King pressed ahead with his plans for the protest at Selma.

On January 18, 1965, King and SNCC's John Lewis led four hundred marchers to the Dallas County Courthouse, obeying all parade requirements, stoplights, and other laws. Although the police observed from the sidelines, they did not interfere with the march and made no arrests. Sheriff Clark's patience reached an end the following day, however, and he arrested sixty-seven people at the courthouse for "unlawful assembly" and "criminal provocation." SCLC continued the marches and 120 people were arrested the next day. Local black educators marched together on January 22 but they avoided arrest for fear of losing their teaching positions. On January 23, Judge Daniel Thomas issued a restraining order against Clark and county officials, and ruled that one hundred applicants could remain at the registrar's office at one time for processing. Clark continued to arrest some protesters at the courthouse.

On February 1, 1965, King and Abernathy decided to go to jail to draw national attention to the protest. Two hundred and sixty-five people marched to the courthouse where they were arrested. While incarcerated, King wrote his "Letter from a Selma, Alabama, Jail" which was published in the *New York Times* on February 5. King's letter made it clear that even though the Civil Rights Act of 1964 had passed, the struggle was not over.

When Judge Thomas issued another injunction against Sheriff Clark, Andrew Young called off further demonstrations, and King left the Selma jail to study the terms of the court order. Henry Wachtel, King's lawyer and friend, began to make arrangements for King to meet with President Johnson and Attorney General Nicholas Katzenbach to discuss the provisions of a Voting Rights Bill. Although King flew to Washington for the meeting, Johnson revealed only that the Justice Department would have an acceptable bill "very soon." When he returned to Selma, King held strategy sessions with SCLC staff. They eventually agreed to accede to

Judge Thomas's request that those wishing to register sign the "appearance book" when they went to the registrar's office in Selma. But they also decided to expand demonstrations into nearby Perry and Lowndes counties.

Following the first night march in Marion, in Perry County, SCLC worker James Orange was arrested by the local police. Fearful for Orange's safety, C. T. Vivian called a mass rally for Zion Chapel Methodist Church on the evening of February 18, 1965, to which more than four hundred people showed up. After several speeches, the audience began to file out of the church, and Police Chief T. O. Harris ordered them to disperse. But as the people tried to leave, the local police charged into the crowd and began beating them. Then, state troopers burst through the rear of the church, beating and clubbing the protestors. A group of blacks ran into a nearby café, and state troopers pursued them and clubbed everyone inside. As they began clubbing Mrs. Viola Jackson, her son Jimmie Lee tried to protect her. The state trooper pulled out his pistol and shot Jackson in the stomach. He died from the wound eight days later.

The police and state troopers also attacked reporters at the scene, destroying their cameras and equipment, and because it was nighttime, there was no good film footage or photographs of the "police riot." The news agencies subsequently condemned the police actions, especially the state troopers under chief Al Lingo. The agencies also registered complaints to Alabama governor George Wallace, who issued no official reprimand but signed an order banning further night marches or protests in Dallas and Perry counties. King at first called for a "Motorcade to Montgomery," the state capital, to protest the police attack and murder, but SCLC staff member James Bevel suggested that people should walk from Selma to Montgomery in protest.

Before leaving Selma, King received an urgent message

MALCOLM X

As the fiery spokesman for the Nation of Islam, Malcolm X criticized both the nonviolent strategies and integrationist objectives of Martin Luther King, Jr., and other civil rights leaders. In the face of unprovoked attacks from whites, Malcolm advocated black self-defense and gained a national and international audience for the separatist movement led by the Honorable Elijah Muhammad. At the end of 1963, however, strains between Malcolm and other Muslim leaders had developed. Jealous of Malcolm's growing influence inside and outside the movement, the other leaders called for increased limits on his public appearances as the primary spokesman for the group. Finally, following the assassination of John F. Kennedy, Malcolm was quoted as saying that it was a case of "chickens coming home to roost." Elijah Muhammad suspended Malcolm for ninety days.

During his suspension, Malcolm made a trip to Mecca, the Islamic holy city, and underwent a significant "conversion experience" in which he gained "new insight into the true religion of Islam, and a better understanding of America's entire racial dilemma." Upon his return, Malcolm officially broke with Elijah Muhammad and the Nation of Islam and set out to establish his own organization, the Organization of Afro-American Unity (OAAU). The new group would reach out to other African-American groups and leaders to create a united front to confront the social, political, and economic problems of people of African descent in the United States and throughout the world.

Following his break with the Nation of Islam, Malcolm, who officially changed his name to El Hadj Malik El Shabazz, was plagued by anonymous death threats, but he continued to make public appearances, sometimes in support of civil rights campaigns in both the North and the South. Before his assassination in February 1965, Malcolm took positions that mirrored those of Martin Luther King, Jr., and even reached out to progressive white groups and individuals in an attempt to make common cause.

from Attorney General Katzenbach that the Justice Department had learned of a conspiracy to assassinate him in Alabama and warned him to be particularly careful about his personal safety. When King returned to Atlanta to prepare for a four-day speaking tour on the West Coast, he heard the news of the assassination of Malcolm X in a hail of gunfire in a ballroom in Harlem. Two members of the Nation of Islam were captured at the scene and later convicted for the murder which many believed was ordered by Malcolm's former mentor, Elijah Muhammad. While King was in Los Angeles speaking to several groups about the need for outside support to bring changes to the deep South, he received the news of the death of Jimmie Lee Jackson in Selma. When asked how he could go on with the increasing violence, murders, and threats against his life, King responded that he had come to grips with this issue early in his public career. "One has to conquer the fear of death if he is going to do anything constructive in life and take a stand against evil."

King returned to Atlanta, and after a short rest left immediately for Selma. In Selma, he met with SCLC officials organizing black communities in Wilcox, Lowndes, and Dallas counties. SNCC members were divided over whether to participate in the proposed march. There were bitter clashes between SNCC and SCLC officials over its advisability, and SNCC leaders finally decided that SNCC would not be an official sponsor, though individual members could participate. King then left for Washington, D.C., to give a speech at Howard University, but was back in Selma the next day to attend Jimmie Lee Jackson's memorial service. In the speech at Howard University and in the eulogy for Jimmie Lee Jackson, King condemned "the timidity of a federal government that is willing to spend millions of dollars a day to defend freedom in Vietnam but cannot protect the rights of its citizens at home." These were King's first public references to the escalating U.S. military commitment in Southeast Asia.

Because of the increasing number of threats on King's life the FBI had unearthed, Attorney General Katzenbach urged him not to lead the march from Selma to Montgomery. When King visited New York City to meet with Bayard Rustin, Harry Wachtel, and other SCLC supporters, he was given round-the-clock police protection, and his friends finally convinced him to limit his participation in the march.

On Saturday, March 6, 1965, Alabama governor George Wallace issued a statement banning the march and authorized the state police to halt it. King and others sent telegrams to the president and attorney general to send federal marshals to protect the marchers because it was clear that State Police Chief Al Lingo meant to enforce Wallace's ban. On Sunday, March 8, approximately six hundred marchers had assembled at Brown Chapel with backpacks and sleeping bags. With SNCC's John Lewis and SCLC's Hosea Williams in the lead, they headed for the Pettus Bridge on the outskirts of Selma.

When the marchers reached the bridge, they were confronted by a cordon of police deputies and state troopers led by Major John Cloud. Many of the troopers were on horseback. Cloud ordered the marchers to disperse in two minutes. As the marchers knelt down to pray, the troopers began to attack them with billy clubs; tear gas was fired into the crowd, and troopers on horseback began to run people down and club them. Those who tried to flee were pursued by the police and beaten. Some were trampled by horses. More than seventy-five people had to be hospitalized following the attack, and John Lewis suffered a concussion.

The "Bloody Sunday" attack on the unarmed marchers on Pettus Bridge had been captured on film by television cameramen, and people who viewed the shocking incident were angered and disturbed. SCLC officials immediately issued a statement that King would lead a second march on Tuesday, March 9, and this time SNCC agreed to be its co-sponsor. A special call went out for clergymen from all over the country to join in the second march, and more than 450 soon arrived in Selma to participate. Meanwhile, SCLC asked U.S. District Judge Frank M. Johnson to set aside Governor Wallace's ban, but Judge Johnson only agreed to hold hearings on Thursday, March 11. Subsequently, President Johnson and other federal officials urged King to postpone the march until after the court hearing.

King was in an extremely difficult position. If he agreed to march in defiance of the ban, he would have to accept responsibility for any violence and injuries that occurred. If King postponed the march, he would damage the movement, throttle its momentum, and leave himself open again to charges that he was unwilling to face the same dangers as his followers. President Johnson sent LeRoy Collins, the director of the Community Relations Service, to Selma to convince King to postpone the march. However, Collins soon realized that postponement was not really an option, given the hundreds of people who had descended on the city to participate. Collins suggested that King lead the marchers to Pettus Bridge and, when confronted by the state troopers, lead the group back to the church. King saw this as a way out of an agonizing dilemma, and Collins promised to convince State Trooper Lingo and Sheriff Clark to cooperate.

On Tuesday morning, hundreds of marchers assembled in Brown Chapel. When King and Abernathy finally emerged from their deliberations, they announced that the march would begin, but gave no indication of what they planned to do. King and Abernathy led the line of 2,000 marchers to the Pettus Bridge, where they were confronted by Lingo, Clark, and the state troopers. U.S. Marshal H. S. Fountain read the order banning the march to King. King then led the marchers up to the state troopers and told them that the marchers wanted to pray. After several prayers, King turned the group around and they headed back to the church singing "We Shall Overcome."

Strong words were exchanged afterward between King and SNCC leaders because King had failed to tell the SCLC and SNCC staff members what he planned to do. King admitted that he had agreed not to defy the court injunction against the march. This admission only further alienated SNCC organizers. SNCC's James Forman denounced this as a "classic example of trickery against the people." But King had little choice, and ultimately he made the right decision because he would have been held in contempt of court had he defied the federal injunction, and would have been held personally responsible for any injuries or deaths that occurred as a result of the "illegal" march.

On Tuesday evening, Rev. James J. Reeb, a minister from Boston, and two others were attacked by a group of white thugs as they were leaving a Selma restaurant. Rev. Reeb received a serious blow to the head and was eventually taken to Birmingham University Hospital, where he died two days later. In cities throughout the country, hundreds of sympathy marches were held to protest the brutal attacks on unarmed protesters in Selma. Following the death of Rev. Reeb, a delegation of clergymen met with President Johnson and urged him to take federal action against the violence and brutality in Alabama. The following day, Saturday, March 13, at his first press conference since "Bloody Sunday," President Johnson urged

Governor Wallace, who was present, to ensure all the citizens of his state the right to vote and to appoint a biracial committee to deal with the pressing social and political issues. Two days later, President Johnson addressed a joint session of Congress and urged members to pass immediately the Voting Rights Bill he had sent them. The measure allowed the attorney general to suspend literacy and other voting requirements, and appoint federal registrars in any state or county where less than half the voting-age population was registered to vote as of November 1, 1964.

While Johnson was addressing the nation, SNCC members and hundreds of black students in Montgomery were clashing with the police. James Forman had organized the students. They conducted marches on the state capital without permits and police tried to disperse them. But the students refused to leave and were viciously attacked with billy clubs, electric prods, and nightsticks. It seemed like "Bloody Sunday" all over again, and the students fled to the nearby black churches. King came to Montgomery and attended a mass rally Saturday night at Beulah Baptist Church at which Forman, using extreme language, threatened to respond violently to future attacks. King ignored Forman's call for militant self-defense and urged the students to participate in the nonviolent march from Selma to Montgomery. However, Forman's growing frustration with nonviolent responses to police violence was shared by many SNCC members, who would soon abandon nonviolence as a tactic altogether.

SCLC moved ahead with the plans for the march. It began at Brown Chapel in Selma on March 21 with 3,200 people led by Martin and Coretta King, Ralph Abernathy, and UN diplomat Ralph Bunche. Despite the presence of federal marshals along Jefferson Davis Highway, the marchers were often accosted by

King leads the march from Selma into Montgomery, Alabama.

white bigots. Segregationists showered the parade route with flyers denouncing King and calling him a "Communist." Nonetheless, freedom songs drowned out the jeers.

King had to leave the march the following day to attend an important speaking engagement in Cleveland, but returned as the demonstrators triumphantly entered Montgomery, their ranks swollen to over 10,000 people. The next morning at the state capitol, protected by more than 800 federal troops, the marchers and protesters cheered, sang, and shouted as King addressed the crowd of over 25,000. He warned those assembled that, "We are still in for a season of suffering in many of the black belt counties of Alabama, many areas of Mississippi, many areas of Louisiana. . . . How long? Not long. Because the arm of the moral universe is long, but it bends toward justice."

The jubilation experienced by those who heard King's beautiful and inspirational message was diminished somewhat when reports began to surface of the shooting of Mrs. Viola Gregg Liuzzo. The Detroit housewife had come to Alabama for the march and had been shot and killed by a carload of Klansmen as she was traveling through Lowndes County with other demonstrators on their way back to Selma. Within days it was announced that four white men had been taken into custody for the shooting. King praised the FBI for its quick action in the case, but it was later revealed that FBI informant Gary Thomas Rowe had been in the car with the Klansmen and had notified authorities of the incident.

While King was extremely disturbed by the killing of Mrs. Liuzzo, the Selma to Montgomery march was one of his greatest successes; and the fact that he was able to attract thousands of whites to this demonstration revealed that he had emerged as a major national leader, not just a black leader. But King felt spiritually weighed down by the overriding question, "What do we do now?" SCLC's Hosea Williams was making plans for launching the "Summer Community Organization and Political Education Project"—SCOPE—which would utilize hundreds of northern college students to work on voter-registration projects. At one point King publicly endorsed the call for a national boycott of Alabama, in which people were asked to refrain from purchasing any products from the state until the violence and discriminatory voting practices ended. However, this suggestion met with great disapproval from King's liberal supporters in the North, and he soon dropped the proposal. But the urban violence and rioting that occurred in the summer of 1965 made it clear that important civil rights issues also needed to be addressed in northern cities.

King had traveled to northern cities on numerous occasions, raising funds for SCLC and the NAACP, and supporting local civil rights leaders and protests. In the spring of 1965, King made several trips to northern cities, beginning with Boston, where he denounced white opposition to court-ordered busing plans. "Some of the same things that are wrong with Alabama are wrong with Boston, Massachusetts," King remarked. King's visits to Philadelphia, New York City, and other northern cities convinced him that SCLC should extend its campaigns north. The blighted conditions in many northern slums, the overcrowded schools, the absence of decent employment, and police brutality seemed to King a formula for explosive actions and reactions that remained unacknowledged by northern politicians and government officials.

On Friday, July 23, King arrived in Chicago for a marathon of speaking engagements, rallies, and meetings. By Sunday evening he had made at least twenty speeches and was completely exhausted. "The doctors tell me I can't get by on two or three hours of sleep a night," King remarked to reporters. Despite his extreme fatigue, King kept up the pace, and even gave a lengthy speech downtown before leading a crowd of 30,000 to City Hall.

King's visit to Chicago was a triumph, and he went on to Cleveland where he spoke in support of black mayoral candidate Carl Stokes. Although the trip to Cleveland did not match Chicago, at least King was welcomed by Cleveland civil rights activists and politicians. In Philadelphia, the next scheduled stop on what was known as the People-to-People Tour, a controversy erupted when local NAACP president Cecil B. Moore, who had been leading demonstrations at the city's Girard College, objected to King's visit. Girard College was a private secondary school located in the heart of the black community in north Philadelphia that refused to allow blacks to attend, citing the stipulation in the will of the founder, early-nineteenth-century merchant Stephen Girard, that the school was to enroll only "poor, white orphan boys." For months Cecil Moore had organized massive demonstrations outside the high granite walls that surrounded the school, but he was not consulted when King was invited to speak there.

Initially, SCLC officials decided to cancel King's visit when Moore stated publicly that King was not welcome in the City of Brotherly Love. However, local civic leaders were outraged by Moore's statements, and finally convinced SCLC staff to reverse the decision. When King arrived on Sunday evening, August 1, 1965, there were more than three hundred enthusiastic supporters at the airport. King told them that "we are not here to establish a movement, but to support the one already here." King kept up a hectic schedule in Philadelphia as well. At Girard College, before a crowd of over 5,000, King compared the walls that surrounded the school to the Berlin Wall in East Germany and accurately predicted that someday it would be torn down, as well as the walls of prejudice at Girard College, by larger freedom movements.

The final stop on his tour was Washington, D.C. (King decided to cancel his visit to New York City due to the strong objections of Harlem's Congressman Adam Clayton Powell, who often referred to himself as "Mr. Civil Rights"). In the nation's capitol, King met with President Johnson to discuss the plans for an upcoming White House Conference on Civil Rights. The next day, August 6, 1965, in the same room in which Abraham Lincoln had signed the Emancipation Proclamation 103 years earlier, King witnessed the signing of the Voting Rights Act of 1965. The new law would guarantee federal protection for the voting rights of hundreds of thousands of previously disenfranchised black southerners. The passage of the Voting Rights Act also signaled the beginning of the end of the successful nonviolent, direct-action protest campaigns most closely associated with Martin Luther King, Jr.

King was in Miami on his way to a much-needed vacation in San Juan, Puerto Rico, when he learned that the disturbances that had begun two days earlier in the Watts section of Los Angeles had escalated. Block upon block of stores had been set on fire with Molotov cocktails and were being looted by mobs as police and National Guardsmen tried to quell the violence. Several church leaders contacted King and asked him to come to Los Angeles to help end the rioting. King was unsure what he could do about the violent situation, and went on to San Juan. But after receiving more dire reports, he changed his plans and flew to Los Angeles where he was joined by Bayard Rustin and Andrew Young. There King met Mayor Sam Yorty, Police Chief William Parker, and Governor Edmund Brown, surveyed the damage in Watts, and spoke at Westminster Community Center, located in a devastated black neighborhood. At Westminster, he was confronted by black militants who heckled him. When he discussed the rioting with a group of teenagers, they kept shouting, "We won! We won!" But King asked them, "How can you say you won when thirty-four Negroes are dead, your community is destroyed, and whites are using the riot as an excuse for inaction?" "We won," they said, "because we made them pay attention to us." King realized that the underlying conditions that had caused the rioting had to be addressed if this kind of violent uprising was to be avoided in the future. King returned to Atlanta more convinced than ever to proceed with SCLC's northern campaigns.

On July 28, 1965, just days before the signing of the Voting Rights Act, President Johnson had announced that he was increasing the number of U.S. troops in Vietnam from 50,000 to 125,000. Although at this time King still considered Johnson a good friend of the civil rights movement, the escalating U.S. military involvement in Vietnam threatened their friendship. Following Johnson's announcement of an increase in U.S. troop strength in Vietnam, King stated that he would send letters to Johnson and the leaders of North and South Vietnam, the Viet Cong, China, and the Soviet Union to urge them to enter into peace negotiations. "I held back until it got to the point that I felt I had to speak out," King told reporters, but he sought no role in peace negotiations or anti-war protests at that time. King did urge others to follow his letter-writing initiative in opposition to the war. President Johnson personally expressed to King in telephone conversations his growing concern over King's public criticism of his Vietnam policy. The president arranged for UN Ambassador Arthur Goldberg to brief King on the U.S. position on September 10, 1965, during King's visit to New York City. While King felt the conversation was productive and friendly, the following day Democratic Senator Thomas Dodd denounced King's public statements calling for peace negotiations and reminded him of the federal criminal statute that banned private citizens from interfering in U.S. foreign policy. King was extremely disturbed by Dodd's public attack—particularly its impact on his civil rights projects—and decided to drop the letter-writing proposal. For the time being, King chose to refrain from public comments on the Vietnam conflict.

In late August 1965, King and the SCLC staff finally agreed that Chicago would be their northern target city, and began making arrangements for King to set up operations in the Windy City. SCLC staff member James Bevel had spent time in Chicago conducting workshops for the Coordinating Council of Community Organizations (CCCO), a coalition of thirty civic, religious, and social groups. Bevel wanted SCLC to become involved in a grassroots movement that would use the collective strength of the poor to negotiate improved conditions from city officials, landlords, merchants, and employers. Jesse Jackson, who joined the SCLC staff during the Selma campaign, was sent to Chicago to serve as the liaison between SCLC and CCCO and to establish Operation Breadbasket. Modeled after Rev. Leon Sullivan's successful Selective Patronage Campaign in Philadelphia, Operation Breadbasket sought to organize the collective purchasing power of the black community to support merchants and businesspersons who provided jobs and services to blacks, and to organize consumer boycotts against noncooperative businesses when necessary.

King decided to live in an impoverished black neighborhood in Chicago and rented an apartment on the West Side. After moving in, King held a meeting at a black church with local residents. They complained about high rents, lack of municipal services, landlord neglect and negligence, and dilapidated and unsanitary conditions. King had heard the same complaints from residents of Watts following the riots, "and if something isn't done in a hurry, we can see a darker night of social disruption."

The Chicago Freedom Movement (CFM) was formed by SCLC, CCCO, and other community-action groups in January 1966. CFM sought to organize the city's poor and work for improvements in housing, employment, and public education. SCLC staff members found it very frustrating to work with the poor residents of Chicago's slums because of their extreme apathy and despair, but they did have some degree of success with the teenage gangs on the West and South sides. James Orange, James Bevel, and Jesse Jackson worked with the Cobras and Blackstone Rangers, two of the largest gangs;

enrolled the teenagers in nonviolent workshops; and held a "gang convention" at Chicago's Palmer House, where King urged over three hundred gang members to stop fighting each other and start working with CFM. Subsequently, some gang members served as marshals at civil rights demonstrations and as King's unofficial bodyguards whenever he was in the city.

King had greater success in winning the support of Chicago's teenage gang members than in gaining the favor of the city's powerful mayor, Richard J. Daley. Daley viewed King and SCLC as outsiders and troublemakers who were undermining Chicago's reputation as the best-run city in the nation. The Daley administration mounted a publicity campaign to counter the CFM's portrait of the conditions in black neighborhoods and showcased its own "anti-slum programs." Many of these programs were run by local black public servants and elected officials who were cogs and wheels in the smooth-running Daley political machine. Moreover, King soon discovered that SCLC would not be able to launch a broad-based program in Chicago because of lack of funds. The SCOPE program in the summer of 1965 had depleted the SCLC's coffers and fund-raising efforts were being hampered by growing competition from other civil rights organizations and groups soliciting money for the expanding peace movement. The lack of focus for the campaigns, as well as the limited funds, diminished SCLC's influence and impact on the lives of Chicago's poor black residents.

While King and SCLC staff members were in Atlanta to make plans for a huge rally in Chicago, they received the news that James Meredith, the first African American to enroll at the University of Mississippi, had been shot while making a highly publicized march from Memphis to Mississippi. The purpose of the march was to encourage intimidated southern blacks to reg-

King takes time to enjoy some pool during his first stay in Chicago.

ister to vote. Unfortunately, on the second day of his march, just inside the Mississippi border, Meredith was ambushed and received two shotgun blasts in the back. King immediately announced that SCLC would take up Meredith's march. North Carolina attorney Floyd McKissick, who became national chairman of CORE in January 1966, and Stokely Carmichael, the new chairman of SNCC, also agreed to take up Meredith's march.

As a result of the continuing violence leveled against SNCC workers and other civil rights activists in Mississippi, Alabama, and other deep South states, many who agreed to participate in this march pledged that they were not going to let what happened to Meredith happen to them. The Meredith March would signal the beginning of a new and much more militant phase of the black struggle for freedom and equality in the United States.

King's funeral, April 9, 1968.

CHAPTER SEVEN

SEE WHAT THE END WILL BE

Martin Luther King, Jr., had not been kept informed by SCLC staff about the significant changes taking place in the southern Black Belt areas while he had been conducting his campaigns in Chicago. King recalled in *Where Do We Go From Here? Chaos or Community*, his last book, that when he arrived in Memphis and traveled to "that desolate spot on Highway 51 where James Meredith had been shot the day before," he heard one of the SNCC activists proclaim, "If one of them damn white Mississippi crackers touches me, I'm gonna knock the hell out of them." This defiant statement reflected the significant changes in consciousness and attitudes toward nonviolence among black southerners and civil rights activists in 1965 and 1966.

Following the successful Selma to Montgomery march, when King shifted SCLC's campaigns to the North and eventually became the driving force behind CFM, a group of SNCC organizers remained in Dallas, Perry, and Lowndes counties in Alabama and participated in the organization of the Lowndes County Freedom Organization (LCFO). Stokely Carmichael, who had graduated from Howard University in 1964, became a full-time SNCC worker in Greenwood, Mississippi, and worked on the Freedom Summer project. Carmichael was a very effective organizer and soon gained the confidence and respect of local black residents. Greatly influenced by the black nationalist ideology most closely associated with Malcolm X, Carmichael, along with other SNCC organizers Bob Mants, Judy Richardson, Scott B. Smith, and Willie Vaughn, worked with a group of militant black farmers in Lowndes County who carried weapons and were determined to defend themselves against any attacks by racist whites.

Given that attempts to register black residents for the Democratic party had resulted in violence, Carmichael investigated the possibility of creating an independent political party. He learned that any independent candidate could gain a position on the election ballot if he or she received 20 percent of the votes in county primary elections. When Carmichael discussed the idea of an independent party with local black residents, they were extremely enthusiastic. Within weeks, a local resident and activist, John Hulett, became chairman of the Lowndes County Freedom Organization (LCFO), whose symbol became the black panther. The LCFO was very successful in gaining the support of the local black residents.

Even though the LCFO was not an all-black political party, King and his SCLC staff in Mississippi viewed its development as misguided and unfortunate. King preferred that newly registered black voters use their political strength to reform the local Democratic party. But there was very little likelihood of such reform taking place. Indeed, die-hard segregationists were making a strong comeback and in the spring of 1966 won the Democratic gubernatorial primaries in Alabama, Mississippi, and Georgia. These results supported Carmichael's contention that neither the Democratic nor the Republican party had much to offer southern black voters. When SNCC members met for their annual meeting in May 1966 in Kingston Springs, Tennessee, the membership was split between those who wanted to continue to advocate nonviolent protests and those who wanted to develop independent black social and political institutions. After several days of stormy debate, Carmichael was able to oust John Lewis from the SNCC chairmanship. Under Carmichael's leadership SNCC became committed to the development of "black consciousness" and urged "all black Americans to begin building independent political, economic, and cultural institutions."

On June 7, 1966, King arrived at Highway 51 outside Memphis at the spot where Meredith had been wounded the day before. He was soon joined by Stokely Carmichael, CORE's new chairman Floyd McKissick, and several dozen others who began marching arm in arm down the highway. Because they had no parade permit, they were hassled by white policemen who followed them in cars, but there was no major incident. Later that evening back in Memphis, King, Carmichael, and McKissick were joined by Roy Wilkins and Whitney Young at Rev. James Lawson's Centenary Methodist Church, where they discussed the plans for the upcoming march.

Roy Wilkins suggested that the march be dedicated to supporting the new civil rights bill then languishing in Congress. Among other things, the new legislation would make attacks on civil rights workers a federal crime. However, Carmichael vehemently objected to this suggestion. He wanted the leaders to issue a "manifesto" emphasizing the importance of ending "black fear" in Mississippi and making it clear that groups not committed to nonviolence would be welcome at the march. Wilkins vehemently objected to Carmichael's proposed manifesto, as well as his abusive language and disrespectful attitude, and stormed out of the meeting, taking Whitney Young with him. King was silent throughout the acrimonious exchange, and Carmichael later admitted that he had purposefully provoked the argument with Wilkins in hopes that Wilkins would leave. Carmichael did not want the NAACP involved in the march and hoped that King would be more amenable to his calls for increased black militancy.

The following morning, Wednesday, June 8, King, Carmichael, and McKissick held a press conference and outlined a slightly toned-down version of Carmichael's manifesto. When Roy Wilkins read the new version, he still found it objectionable and refused to endorse it. Later that day King, Carmichael, and McKissick led the columns of marchers on Highway 51, but King soon had to leave to make a two-day trip to Chicago. While King was away, Carmichael and McKissick got SCLC staff member Robert Green to agree to change the route of the march: They would leave Highway 51 and head toward Greenwood, in the Delta region. Over the next several days the marchers made their way toward Greenwood, SNCC's stronghold, and when the marchers entered the town on Thursday, June 16, King was still in Chicago.

SCLC staff agreed to let SNCC take charge of the arrangements in Greenwood, and plans were made for the marchers to pitch tents in the school yard of the Stone Street Negro Elementary School. However, the local police commissioner, B. A. Hammond, soon arrived and told the marchers that they were trespassing. Carmichael objected and he and two others

On Highway 51, where protester James Meredith had been shot days earlier.

were arrested and taken away to jail. The marchers left the school yard and went to Broad Street Park, where they planned a rally and received a permit to pitch their tents. Carmichael was released on bond after several hours and went directly to the park, where the rally had begun. "This is the twenty-seventh time I've been arrested," he angrily told the crowd. "I ain't gonna be arrested no more. . . . [Police Chief] Buff Hammond has to go. I'm gonna tell you baby, that the only way we're gonna get justice is when we have a black sheriff. . . . Every courthouse in Mississippi should be burnt down tomorrow so we can get rid of the dirt." SNCC organizer Willie Ricks shouted to Carmichael, "What do we want?" "Black Power," was his response. "When do we want it?" "Now!" Soon the blacks in the crowd joined in, "We want Black Power! We want Black Power!"

"Black Power" as a slogan spread throughout the country through newspaper and television reports, but it also caused a split within the ranks of the marchers. King, upon his arrival the next day, was so concerned that he called a meeting with McKissick and Carmichael to discuss the slogan's implications. At a small Catholic parish house in Yazoo City, Mississippi, King made clear his misgivings about the Black Power slogan, particularly the "implications of violence the press had already attached to the phrase." Carmichael and McKissick, however, were united in their defense of Black Power and argued that "power is the only thing respected in this world, and we must get it at any cost." King agreed that "we must use every constructive means to amass economic and political power. This is the kind of legitimate power we need. . . . But this must come through a program, not merely through a slogan." Carmichael and McKissick considered the slogan important as a "rallying cry," just like "Freedom Now"; however, their objective was also to raise the consciousness of black people. Carmichael and McKissick were adamant about using the phrase, and Carmichael confessed to King that he had used King to provide a forum for the slogan's introduction and to force King to take a stand on Black Power. Upon hearing this, King told Carmichael, "I've been used before."

When the marchers reached Philadelphia, Mississippi, where the bodies of Chaney, Goodman, and Schwerner had been found in 1964, King tried to lead a memorial service, but his words were drowned out by a white mob that surrounded them. The whites attacked the marchers with ax handles, clubs, and hoes as the police looked the other way. It was only when the marchers fought back that the police, led by Sheriff Lawrence Rainey, decided to drive the whites away. Later that evening, shots were exchanged between white vigilantes and armed marchers. King telegraphed the White House request-ing federal protection, but there was no response.

It was raining heavily when the marchers reached Canton, Mississippi, and began pitching their tents in the yard of a black school, McNeil Elementary. Police and state troopers soon appeared and, without warning, began firing tear gas into the school yard. Although no one was seriously injured, this was the most serious police attack on unarmed marchers since "Bloody Sunday" in Selma. King again telegraphed the White House to request federal marshals, but again got no response, probably because of King's earlier public statements criticiz-ing President Johnson's Vietnam policy. Before going on to Jackson, King led three hundred nonviolent marchers back to Philadelphia, just to show the whites that they were not afraid. They were again confronted by Sheriff Lawrence Rainey, who told them that they could not assemble on the courthouse steps. King and Abernathy knelt and prayed, and although a crowd of whites gathered, the black leaders were able to get the marchers out of town without incident.

"I had expected some hostility. . ."

After twenty-seven days, the Meredith March finally reached Jackson, and over 12,000 people gathered on the capitol grounds to hear the speeches delivered by King, Carmichael, and McKissick. Given the brutal attacks on the unarmed marchers and the divisions generated over the "Black Power" slogan, the Meredith March raised more issues than it settled for King and his SCLC staff. All they knew was that they were tired and disturbed by the events in Mississippi and were ready to return to Chicago.

King was hopeful that the campaign in Chicago would serve to vindicate his continued commitment to nonviolence. Plans were being made for a massive "Freedom Sunday" rally and march on City Hall. CFM leaders hoped to attract 100,000 demonstrators to the protest. However, when King taped their demands to the doors at City Hall, it was 98 degrees in the shade and the city was in the midst of a terrible heat wave. It was estimated that only about 30,000 marchers participated in the rally. The next day, when King went to City Hall to present the demands in person, a noticeably irritated Mayor Daley rejected them, claiming Chicago already had an effective slum-clearance program.

In an attempt to cool off from the stifling heat, young people had opened fire hydrants throughout the city. Fearing the loss of water pressure necessary to fight fires, the fire commissioner ordered police to turn them off. On Monday, July 12, 1966, when police came to a West Side neighborhood to turn off a fire hydrant, a fight broke out between the police and some gang members. The incident touched off widespread rioting and looting. More than twenty people were injured and scores were arrested. The following day King and his associates held a meeting at a black church with gang leaders who described incidents of police brutality and their plans for retaliation. King told reporters that there was a need for a civilian review board to investigate the actions by and complaints against the police. That evening rioting erupted again and was even more violent and widespread. The next morning King toured the riot-torn areas, pleading with the young people to stay at home, but that night witnessed the most brutal confrontations yet between police and rioters. Snipers exchanged shots with police from rooftops and teenagers firebombed stores. Illinois Governor Otto Kerner sent 4,000 National Guardsmen to Chicago and they began patrolling the streets in jeeps and trucks, carrying loaded rifles. Order was finally restored, but over the four days of rioting, two people were killed, over two hundred and fifty people were injured, and hundreds were jailed.

At a press conference following the rioting, an angry and frustrated Mayor Daley lashed out at anarchists, Communists, and SCLC for coming to the city and "promoting violence" among the teenagers. SCLC staff member James Bevel had shown several gang members a film of the Watts riot the year before, but merely to illustrate the futility and self-defeating aspects of riots and violence. King subsequently met with Daley and challenged the mayor's remarks, since it was well known that King and his staff were in the streets throughout the riot trying to prevent violent and destructive actions. Daley later retracted his statement and finally agreed to have sprinklers attached to fire hydrants so that children could escape the heat. He later appointed a citizens committee to investigate police practices.

King and CFM leaders had consistently complained about housing discrimination in the city and throughout Cook County, but fierce opposition from the real estate industry prevented the passage by the state legislature of open housing laws. On July 13, 1966, however, Gov. Otto Kerner issued an executive order that attempted to address the problem. State officials were to refuse licenses to real estate agents found guilty of racial, ethnic, or religious discrimination. The executive order served as a major justification for a SCLC protest, led by James Bevel, against a real estate agency in Gage Park in the southwestern section of Chicago that had consistently discriminated against blacks seeking homes in the area. Unfortunately, the protest at the real estate agency was broken up when the demonstrators were attacked by a white mob. This attack served as one rationale for King's announcement of a series of open housing marches in southwest Chicago and the adjacent suburbs.

The first series of marches, led by Al Raby, James Bevel, and Jesse Jackson, took place on July 30 and 31. The black and white demonstrators were confronted by mobs of jeering whites who hurled rocks, bottles, and other debris. Many marchers were injured, including Jackson and Raby; CFM leaders complained about the lack of protection from the police, who were nowhere to be seen. In the next series of marches the police were present and even engaged in pitched battles with the white mobs, but many demonstrators were injured by rocks and bottles. On August 5, 1966, King headed a march into Marquette Park and although more than 1,000 policemen were present, the marchers were showered with rocks and bottles. King was knocked to his knees by a rock. Police and reporters rushed to his side. "I had expected some hostility," King said, visibly shaken, "but not of this enormity." The angry mobs followed the marchers and by the end of the day over thirty people were injured and forty-one arrested.

Mayor Daley wanted the marches to end and sent several black lieutenants to meet with King and Raby, but nothing significant was offered or settled. While King was attending the SCLC annual meeting in Jackson, Mississippi, in which the organization restated its commitment to remain in Chicago, Daley sent CFM leaders a letter offering to provide funds for "urban renewal" programs and improved housing and jobs for black Chicagoans in return for ending the marches. This inconsequential offer was quickly rejected. Then, on August 8,

Racist protesters pelted King with rocks when he marched through Chicago's southwest section.

without prior agreement from other CFM leaders, Jesse Jackson announced that additional marches would be held in the Bogan section of Chicago and in nearby Cicero, two areas that prided themselves on being "for whites only." With this new announcement, Roman Catholic Archbishop John Cody, who had previously denounced discriminatory housing practices, joined the chorus of Chicago's black and white leaders calling for an end to the marches.

Jackson, Raby, and Bevel rejected Archbishop Cody's appeal, and held a demonstration in downtown Chicago in front of the offices of the Chicago Real Estate Board, the leaders of which consistently defended racially discriminatory practices by realtors. They also led hundreds of black and white marchers into three all-white neighborhoods, where more angry whites confronted them. Although no date was set for the Cicero march, Cook County sheriff Richard B. Ogilvie, fearing widespread violence and injury, promised to use every legal means to prevent any demonstrations there. The latest series of marches had stretched police resources to the limit, and with the Cicero demonstration in the offing, Daley was desperate to end the marches. The mayor soon convinced Episcopal Bishop James Montgomery and other influential members of the Conference on Religion and Race to sponsor a "summit conference" that would address CFM demands. Headed by well-respected industrialist Ben Heineman, the conference was held on Wednesday, August 17, at the diocesan offices for the Episcopal Church.

King and CFM leaders wanted effective fair housing legislation that would punish real estate agents who discriminated against racial and ethnic minorities seeking to rent or purchase homes and apartments. The members of the Chicago Real Estate Board refused to support such legislation, and argued that realtors had to follow the dictates of their clients. King made it clear that this was the same argument restaurant and hotel owners made to oppose laws calling for nondiscrimination in public accommodations, and since the passage of the 1964 Civil Rights Act, there was no evidence that southern white businesses had suffered any adverse impact due to desegregation. Daley prodded the representatives of the Real Estate Board to come up with a statement supporting open housing legislation in Chicago, but CFM members found it unsatisfactory. However, they did accept Ben Heineman's recommendation that a subcommittee be appointed to work out an acceptable statement.

Two days after the summit meeting, city officials obtained an injunction against the CFM, restricting protest marches in Chicago to one a day with no more than five hundred participants. Rather than defy the injunction, the CFM held demonstrations beyond the city limits, and King led a march into all-white South Deering, where white mobs again clashed with police. CFM also set the date for the march into Cicero, August 27, and began meeting with state and local police officials to work out the details. However, when the summit conference reconvened on August 26, King and Raby decided to accept the ten-point agreement submitted by the subcommittee headed by Bishop Montgomery. Among other things, the agreement contained statements that committed the Chicago Real Estate Board, Housing Authority, and Commission on Human Relations to a policy of "fair housing." King told reporters following the meeting that the agreement was "far-reaching and creative" and served as a "solid vindication of southern-style protest in a northern city."

Before the ink was dry on the signatures to the agreement, however, journalists and civil rights activists began pointing out its flaws and weaknesses. For example, although the Chicago Real Estate Board accepted the "philosophy" of open housing, it maintained its right "to criticize details . . . in open occupancy legislation at the state level." While the Commission on Human Relations stated its commitment to enforce the city's Fair Housing Ordinance, it would do so "without placing undue burden's on any [real estate] broker's business." In the case of the mortgage and lending agencies, they merely reiterated earlier statements about their commitment to "non-discriminatory" practices. Although pledges were made by CFM leaders to follow up on the agreement, the leaders made little progress due to increasing divisions within CFM's ranks.

Some commentators have suggested that King had snatched defeat from the jaws of victory in Chicago by agreeing to the terms in the settlement and calling off the marches. But it is also likely that King believed that he was dealing with honorable men who would live up to their promises and commitments. More important, King's decision in Chicago was consistent with decisions he had made in the past. While he would have been willing to march into Cicero, he was unwilling to take responsibility for leading an illegal march in which many people would likely face injury and even death. King's moral commitment to nonviolence defined his behavior in Selma, Alabama; Greenwood, Mississippi; and Chicago; and while he was willing to sacrifice his life for his principles, he was also committed to saving lives as part of his commitment to social change. King's commitment to saving lives also helps explain his outspoken opposition to the war in Vietnam.

⊰ ⊰ ⊰

"*. . . time to break the silence.*"

After the overwhelmingly negative response to his initial foray into the controversy developing nationally by 1965 over

VIETNAM AND BLACK AMERICANS

As the U.S. involvement in the civil war in South Vietnam expanded, the number of African Americans in combat units increased greatly, and complaints began to be voiced by black leaders. Some even made the argument that black troops were being used as "cannon fodder" in the war because there were so few employment opportunities available in civilian society. Black soldiers in Vietnam were aware of the civil rights protests taking place in the United States and likened the U.S. oppression of the Vietnamese people to the racial oppression at home. In August 1965, when Martin Luther King, Jr., first criticized the mounting U.S. role in Vietnam, black public opinion was generally supportive of the U.S. military action. However, as the number of combat troops increased and the casualty lists grew longer, African Americans, along with others, began to ask, "Why are we in Vietnam?"

Black complaints about the war were also fueled by reports of discriminatory treatment toward black military personnel in Vietnam. The military justice system came under particular attack because punishments of black soldiers were invariably more severe than those given white soldiers convicted of the same offenses. Black soldiers complained that they were not receiving training in areas that would prepare them for employment in the civilian job market. Within the armed forces, blacks were significantly underrepresented in the higher ranks of commissioned and noncommissioned officers.

With the advent of Black Power and the coming of the black consciousness movement, black soldiers began to ask to be allowed to wear Afro hairstyles, to be served soul food, and to be allowed to listen to soul music. These demands escalated after the assassination of Martin Luther King, Jr., and black soldiers were even less likely to tolerate racist statements and treatment by white officers and enlisted men. On some military installations racial incidents escalated into open warfare between black and white troops.

After 1969, military leaders became more sympathetic toward black demands for change in the military's policies and practices, but improvements were slow in coming for black soldiers in Vietnam.

the Johnson administration's increasing military commitments in Vietnam, King made few public statements about the war. In some of his sermons, he questioned the morality of U.S. involvement and urged young men who opposed the war on moral grounds to apply for "conscientious objector" status when drafted. In the November 1966 elections, former SNCC organizer Julian Bond won election to the Georgia state legislature from a predominantly black district in Atlanta. When Bond sought to take his seat in the state legislature, the other representatives voted to deny Bond his seat because he had publicly endorsed anti-Vietnam statements issued by Stokely Carmichael and other SNCC leaders. In numerous speeches in December 1966 and January 1967, King publicly supported Bond's right to dissent against the administration's Vietnam policies and to be seated in the Georgia legislature.

Many of King's friends and advisors, including Stanley Levison, Henry Wachtel, and Bayard Rustin, as well as civil rights leaders Roy Wilkins and Whitney Young, counseled him to avoid the war issue because it would alienate the president and other politically powerful individuals and thereby severely damage the civil rights cause. However, by January 1967 King had come to the conclusion that the civil rights cause had already been damaged severely by splits over Black Power and the increasing white backlash. At the same time, the expanding military commitment in Vietnam had begun to seriously affect the federal government's funding for the War on Poverty.

By the end of March 1967 he had made his decision to speak out against the war and a few days later, on April 4, 1967, he addressed an overflowing audience at New York City's Riverside Church, declaring that it was "time to break the silence." In one of his most important speeches, King described in detail the history of U.S. involvement in Vietnam and the Johnson administration's steadily escalating commitment of arms and troops, and why he had to speak out against the war.

King called for an end to all bombing in North and South Vietnam; a unilateral cease-fire by U.S. troops; recognition of the National Liberation Front, the political arm of the Viet Cong guerrilla movement, as a legitimate participant in any peace negotiations; and the setting of a specific date for the removal of all foreign troops from Vietnam in accordance with the 1954 Geneva Agreement.

As he had predicted, King's speech was denounced in pulpits and the press across the country, and disavowed by other civil rights leaders. While King was surprised by the strength of the criticism that came from individuals and institutions he felt would be sympathetic, he felt relieved by what he had done. King continued to speak out against the war throughout the year, including giving a series of lectures broadcast by the Canadian Broadcasting Corporation in November and December, later published in book form as *The Trumpet of Conscience*. By fall 1967 anti-war leaders and activists began consideration of a political challenge to Johnson's Vietnam policies and debated whether to form a third political party or mount an attack from within the Democratic party. King was asked if he would be willing to be the anti-war party's candidate for president in 1968, and while he was flattered, King said he was not interested in becoming a politician.

King continued to pursue pressing civil rights commitments throughout the remainder of 1967. In Louisville, Kentucky, SCLC staff had supported the effort of the Ad Hoc Committee on Open Housing in lobbying the Louisville City Council to pass legislation guaranteeing nondiscrimination in housing.

Unfortunately, the Council voted down open housing legislation on April 11, 1967, and for seven weeks SCLC and the Ad Hoc Committee mounted protests and marches, and threatened to disrupt the running of the Kentucky Derby. Although National Guardsmen protected the racetrack on Derby Day, May 6, 1967, the marches continued throughout the month, only to fizzle out at the beginning of June. SCLC and the Ad Hoc Housing Committee decided to concentrate its efforts on a voter-registration campaign to vote out of office the council members opposed to open housing.

In June 1967, more and more SCLC members were sent to Cleveland to assist Carl Stokes's campaign for mayor. King understood that among the important vehicles for bringing about social and economic change were voter-registration campaigns and the mobilization of black communities in support of political candidates responsive to the needs of the poor.

Despite the civil rights demonstrations and the abbreviated War on Poverty, the conditions for the rural and urban poor, black and white, had not greatly improved. Marion Wright, an attorney working with the NAACP Legal Defense Fund, suggested that King gather a group of poor people, black and white, from Mississippi and take them to Washington, D.C., to protest the federal government's failure to deal effectively with the national problem of persistent poverty.

At the SCLC retreat in Warrenton, Virginia, in September 1967, the issue was debated for an entire week. The most insistent opposition to the idea of launching a "Poor People's Campaign" came from Jesse Jackson, who headed SCLC's Operation Breadbasket. The effectiveness of Jackson's boycott campaigns in Chicago to force white-owned companies to hire black workers and buy from black businesses had led King in July 1967 to announce that Operation Breadbasket would be expanded into a national program. At the same time, however, King had also come to feel that, given the depth of the problems of joblessness and poverty in the United States, it would require "socialistic" approaches to solve them. It would be necessary for the federal government to intervene in the provision of jobs and housing where the private sector proved inadequate. King tried to convince Jackson that capitalism, especially "black capitalism," was not up to the task of solving the problems of poverty and joblessness in black communities.

Out of the Warrenton retreat came SCLC's commitment to the Poor People's Campaign, but it would be a daunting task to carry out because King envisioned a national protest that included the Mexican-American, Native American, and Appalachian white as well as the African-American poor. King reorganized the SCLC offices and appointed Bob Rutherford as the new executive director to begin planning the project. King traveled around the country speaking to various groups about the need for the federal government to do more for the poor, especially the black poor. In articles and editorials on the Poor People's Campaign, however, conservative writers argued that King was calling on the federal government to give "preferential treatment" and special privileges to African Americans and others in poverty, which was contrary to the traditional American ethos of "rugged individualism," and that African Americans and others in poverty needed to "pull themselves up by their own bootstraps."

King responded to these conservative critics by pointing out that no white group had pulled itself out of poverty without assistance from the government. The early white settlers received free land from the government, and since that time white farmers, industrialists, and other businessmen have been dependent on the federal government to insure adequate profits. "When [federal assistance] is given to white people, it's called a subsidy," King explained. "Everybody in this country is on welfare. Suburbia was built by federally subsidized credits. And the highways were built by federally subsidized firms to the tune of ninety percent." While the poor are told that they need to be "rugged individualists," the federal government is providing "socialism for the rich."

King had been calling for compensatory programs to assist the black and white poor in their social and economic advancement for many years. In *Why We Can't Wait*, he recommended the passage of a "Bill of Rights for the Disadvantaged" to compensate for the social and economic deprivations. In *Where Do We Go From Here? Chaos or Community*, King emphasized his belief that "it is morally right to insist that every person have a decent house, and adequate education and enough money to provide basic necessities for one's family." It would require "discipline, understanding, organization, and sacrifice" to achieve these goals, and might require "a radical restructuring of the architecture of American society."

The Poor People's Campaign was conceived as a way of dramatizing the plight of the poor and the need for radical economic restructuring, but King had difficulty convincing even the SCLC staff that the campaign represented the best way to achieve this objective. In the past, marchers were recruited from local protest movements. From where were the marchers going to be recruited for the Poor People's Campaign? And for those who participated, what would they come away with? King believed that those who attended the march would be given hope, courage, and an "inner power" to face the future. The response of the press and government officials ranged from mildly supportive to vehemently opposed.

Some critics predicted that the Poor People's March would result in riots and destruction to the nation's capitol, and many condemned King for even suggesting such a project.

The negative responses to the Poor People's Campaign only added to the extreme depression King was suffering from at the end of 1967 and beginning of 1968. In public, members of his audience were unable to detect any changes in his passion and eloquence, but his close friends worried about his state of mind. King had received death threats throughout his public career and had learned to live with them. However, by the fall of 1967 the threats had become more ominous and were beginning to take their toll. The FBI continued its disinformation campaign, spreading stories that King was involved with Communist conspiracies, sexual affairs, and embezzlement of SCLC funds. King and SCLC were also targeted by the FBI's COINTELPRO program, which FBI directors designed to bring about the destruction of "black nationalist hate groups" operating in the United States. While it was later revealed that right-wing fanatics had put out a contract on his life, at the time King was unaware of it. Nonetheless King and his SCLC assistants felt that he was being stalked. In January 1968, King sent field agents to Baltimore, Philadelphia, Newark, Boston, and other cities to recruit groups and individuals to participate in the Poor People's March, but they were not having much success. "We're in terrible shape with this poor people's campaign," an apprehensive King told a staff member in early February, "It just isn't working. People aren't responding."

In this depressed state King delivered one of his most moving sermons to his Ebenezer congregation on February 4, 1968. King discussed his own death and eulogy: "If any of you are around when I have to meet my day, I don't want a long funeral." He did not want the eulogist to mention his numerous awards and honors, but merely to mention "that Martin Luther King, Jr., tried to give his life serving others," that "he tried to be right on the war question," that he tried to feed the hungry and clothe the naked. "Yes, if you want to say that I was a drum major, say that I was a drum major for justice. Say I was a drum major for peace. That I was a drum major for righteousness."

In early March 1968, James Lawson, a longtime friend and pastor of the Centenary Methodist Church in Memphis, contacted King and pleaded with him to come to Memphis. In February, the sanitation workers, who were almost all black, went on strike demanding that local officials recognize their branch of the American Federation of State, County, and Municipal Workers Union as their bargaining agent and grant them a contract guaranteeing higher wages and improved working conditions. Not only did the administration of Mayor Henry Leob refuse to recognize the union, Leob also threatened to fire all striking workers. When a local support committee was formed, called the Community on the Move for Equality (COME), and began staging marches in support of the striking workers, city officials went to the local courts and received an injunction banning further demonstrations. Rev. Lawson, a member of COME, wanted King to address a rally on March 18 in support of the striking black workers.

While accepting Lawson's invitation would divert King from his speaking tour for the Poor People's Campaign, he decided to go to Memphis because the sanitation workers' strike represented precisely the kind of economic issue he had been addressing over the past few years. King and his assistants arrived at the Lorraine Motel, a black hotel, and made their way to the Masonic Temple, where over 17,000 people were waiting. King's address fired up the huge crowd. "We are tired of being on the bottom," he proclaimed to his enthusiastic audience.

"We are tired of working our hands off and laboring every day and not even making a wage adequate for the daily basic necessities of life." King called for a massive march downtown on March 22, "and we aren't gonna let any injunction turn us around."

King left Memphis for Mississippi to continue his speaking tour for the Poor People's Campaign. He returned to Memphis for a planning and strategy session on March 21. However, a late winter blizzard hit Memphis, necessitating the rescheduling of the march to the 28th. During his several visits to Memphis, local black leaders never mentioned that militant black nationalist groups in the city had called for violent, disruptive action in support of the striking black workers. On Thursday, March 28, when King and his assistants arrived in Memphis, there were over 6,000 people waiting. The crowd started down Main Street at about 11:00 A.M. with King and Abernathy and James Lawson in the lead. As they were walking, they began to hear the sound of crashing glass: Black teenagers at the back of the column had begun breaking store windows and looting the contents. Sirens and alarms went off, and King saw ahead of him a line of policemen in full riot gear. King told Lawson to have the marchers return to the church saying, "I will never lead a violent march."

Bernard Lee, King's assistant, stopped a car and convinced the driver to take them back to the Lorraine Motel, but the streets were blocked. In the downtown area clashes between police and rioters had erupted, and gun shots were being exchanged. King was taken to the Rivermont Holiday Inn on the Mississippi River. Before the violence ended that day, over 155 stores were looted, one black teenager was killed and twenty were injured. The National Guard was brought in to patrol the city. In the hotel room, King was extremely upset and felt guilty about the outbreak of violence; it was the first time that marchers he led had resorted to rioting. When King was told that a youth gang, the Invaders, had threatened violence during the march, he was even more upset. Why hadn't he been told?

King was depressed and disturbed about the violence. He knew he would have to meet with reporters later, but he could not sleep or even rest for worrying about what this would mean for future marches, especially the Poor People's Campaign. Later that evening three members of the Invaders arrived at King's hotel room and asked to speak with him. At first King told Abernathy to talk with them, but they angrily refused to leave without speaking to King. He came out and the young gang members explained that the local leaders had refused to allow them to participate in the strike actions, and rejected their offers of assistance. King told the gang members he would return to the city to lead a nonviolent demonstration, and he wanted to meet with them about it.

King returned to Atlanta, but when he called a meeting of the SCLC staff on Saturday, March 30, he was still clearly disturbed by the events in Memphis, and when Jesse Jackson and others began to question what this meant for the Poor People's Campaign, King walked out. He later told them to go ahead with the plans for the march in Memphis now scheduled for Friday, April 5. The next day King went to Washington, D.C., to fulfill a long-standing commitment to preach at the Episcopal Cathedral. That Sunday evening President Johnson made a televised address to the nation in which he announced a reduction in the bombing in Vietnam. He also said he was disturbed by the divisions the war was causing in the country. At the end of his speech, President Johnson declared that he would not seek another term as president.

King, like most people throughout the nation, was astounded.

Senator Eugene McCarthy's challenge in New Hampshire, where he came in second in the Democratic primary, had been followed by Senator Robert Kennedy's announcement that he too was a candidate for the presidency and that he would run in opposition to Johnson's Vietnam policies. While these candidacies were viewed as serious threats to his renomination, virtually no one expected that Johnson would drop out of the race. After the announcement, friends and supporters contacted King and congratulated him on his triumph. Many people had come to believe that it was King's principled opposition to the Vietnam War that laid the groundwork for Johnson's decision not to run again for the presidency.

Johnson's announcement buoyed King's sagging spirits as plans were being made for his return to Memphis on Wednesday, April 3. When he arrived, there were a number of policemen present because of reports that King had received more threats on his life. King never felt really secure surrounded by police, and asked to be taken straight to the Lorraine Motel. He spent the entire afternoon in meetings with SCLC staff and local leaders. Several lawyers present were planning the challenge to the injunction issued against the march, but King intended to march whether or not the injunction was lifted.

That evening, an exhausted King returned to his hotel room as rain and wind swirled outside. Tornado warnings had been issued for the Memphis area. King was resting in his room when Abernathy called and said that there were cameras, reporters, and over 2,000 people at the Masonic Temple. Abernathy urged King to at least put in an appearance. Because he felt it would generate support for the march on Friday, King dressed and went out into the driving storm. The building was filled with people and cameras began flashing as King mounted the platform. He was introduced by Abernathy.

"I am delighted to see each of you tonight in spite of the storm warning. You reveal that you are determined to go on anyhow. Something is happening in Memphis, something is happening in our world." King surveyed world history. He declared that he was glad to be living in the second half of the twentieth century when movements for freedom and liberation were flourishing throughout the world. He described the conditions in Memphis and city officials' refusal to grant the black sanitation workers union representation and a decent wage. He was happy he did not sneeze that day in Harlem when the deranged woman stabbed him with the letter opener, he said, because had he sneezed, he would have died and would not have witnessed the changes that had taken place since 1958 and he would not be part of the movement to support the sanitation workers' cause.

King then mentioned the threats on his life coming from "our sick white brothers." But these threats did not matter.

> [God's] allowed me to go up to the mountaintop.
> And I've looked over. And I've seen the promised
> land. I may not get there with you. But I want you
> to know tonight, that we, as a people will get to the
> promised land.

Those present, especially King's friends and staff members, were unnerved by his words. Andrew Young recalled that "we were all awed and shaken by Martin's speech. But Martin seemed to be buoyed by inspiration." After the rally King and his assistants went to the home of Rev. Benjamin Hooks. When they returned to the Lorraine Motel, King was pleasantly surprised to find that his brother A.D. had arrived from Florida. They stayed up talking till 3:00 A.M.

The next morning King awoke late and met with his staff to

The day before the assassination at the Lorraine Motel, Memphis, Tennessee.

go over plans for the march. King and Abernathy had lunch in the hotel room and afterward King visited with his brother A.D. They had been invited to dinner that evening at the home of Rev. Samuel Kyles, where King had enjoyed Mrs. Kyles's soul food dinners on many occasions. Before dressing to leave, Andrew Young and James Lawson arrived to announce that the local judge had agreed to lift the injunction and allow the march to take place on Monday, April 8. King was delighted at the news and finished dressing. He then stepped out on to the hotel balcony, talked to Rev. Kyles, and, spotting Jesse Jackson below, invited Jackson to join them. When Abernathy went back to the hotel room to get King's topcoat, King stood alone on the balcony, looking over the railing.

Then several shots rang out. King was struck in the face and throat, he grabbed his neck and fell to the balcony floor. As Abernathy emerged from the hotel room, he saw that King had been shot and rushed over and cradled King in his arms. Andrew Young rushed over and felt for a pulse. There was none. The hotel courtyard soon filled with police. The ambulance arrived and King was placed on a stretcher and raced to St. Joseph's Hospital. In the hospital emergency room, the doctors and nurses worked feverishly, massaging King's heart, attaching tubes. Finally, a surgeon came out of the emergency room and told Abernathy that it was over.

King had been shot in the face and right jaw by a bullet fired from a high-powered rifle. Later, federal agents received reports that following the shooting a white man was seen racing away from the murder area in a white Mustang. They subsequently found a .30-06 rifle in a doorway and James Earl Ray, an escaped convict, was eventually convicted of the assassination.

When news of King's assassination was broadcast, rioting and violence erupted in 110 cities in the United States. Thirty-nine people were killed and over 14,000 were arrested. The worst violence took place in Washington, D.C., where over 700 fires were set and 10 people were reported killed. An estimated 75,000 federal troops and National Guardsmen were called out to restore order and patrol riot areas.

President Johnson declared Sunday, April 7, as the official day of mourning. People from all over the world sent telegrams and letters of condolence to Coretta and the King family in Atlanta. In Memphis, on Monday, April 8, Abernathy, Coretta Scott King, and three of her children led over 20,000 people in the nonviolent march in support of the striking sanitation workers. Within eight days Memphis city officials agreed to

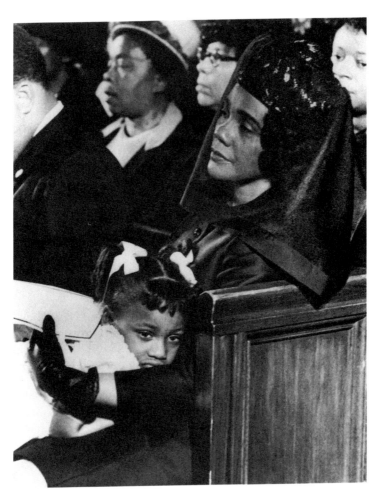

Coretta Scott King and daughter Bernice at King's funeral.

recognize the sanitation workers' union and eventually negotiated wage increases and other benefits.

King's funeral took place on Tuesday, April 9, at Ebenezer Baptist Church in Atlanta. It was estimated that as many as 80,000 people surrounded the church. Among the friends and dignitaries present were Harry Belafonte, Thurgood Marshall,

Robert Kennedy, Jacqueline Kennedy, Eugene McCarthy, Ramsey Clark, and Richard Nixon. Conspicuous in his absence was Lyndon Johnson, who sent Vice President Hubert Humphrey as his representative. Members of the SCLC staff and other civil rights leaders were present, and following a brief eulogy, Coretta requested that a tape of King's speech, "A Drum Major for Justice," be played.

On the day of King's burial, a House committee agreed to accept the Senate's version of the Civil Rights Bill then pending in Congress. Despite the long-standing opposition of the National Association of Real Estate Boards and other housing organizations, the bill passed the House on April 10. The Civil Rights Law of 1968 outlawed discriminatory practices that prevented African Americans and other minorities from obtaining housing in neighborhoods of their own choosing.

Martin Luther King, Jr., dedicated his life to the cause of racial and economic justice and sought the creation of the Beloved Community. His message and vision for American society, given its long history of slavery, oppression, racism, and economic inequality, provides essential information for present and future generations who understand the need "to redeem the soul of America."

CHRONOLOGY

1929   January 15: Born in Atlanta, Georgia

1942   Fall: Enters tenth grade at Booker T. Washington
           High School

1944   Fall: Enrolls at Morehouse College

1947   Preaches trial sermon at Ebenezer Baptist Church

1948   February 25: Ordained in the Baptist ministry

           April: Admitted to Crozer Theological Seminary

           June: Receives B.A. in sociology from Morehouse
               College

           Fall: Assigned to a student pastorate at First Baptist
               Church of East Elmhurst in Queens, New York

1951   May 8: Receives Bachelor of Divinity degree, the Pearl
               Plafker Memorial Award, and the J. Lewis Crozer
               Fellowship from Crozer Theological Seminary.

           September: Enrolls in the Ph.D. program in
               Systematic Theology at Boston University

1952   February: Meets Coretta Scott

1953   June 18: Marries Coretta Scott in Marion, Alabama

1954   April: Accepts pastorate at the Dexter Avenue
               Baptist Church in Montgomery, Alabama

1955   June 5: Receives Ph.D. from Boston University

           August: Joins the NAACP branch's executive
               committee

           November 17: Daughter, Yolanda Denise, is born

December 1: Rosa Parks is arrested after she refuses to give up her seat on the bus to a white passenger

December 5: Citywide boycott of Montgomery bus system begins

1956: January: Arrested, convicted, and fined for driving five miles over the speed limit

January 30: King home is bombed

February 21: Arrested for organizing the bus boycott

May 11: U.S. Supreme Court rules in *Browder v. Gayle*, declares the bus segregation law unconstitutional

1957 May 17: Attends the "Prayer Pilgrimage" in Washington, D.C., and delivers first national address

July: Receives NAACP's Spingarn Award

August: The first conference of the Southern Christian Leadership Conference (SCLC) is held in Atlanta

October 23: Son, Martin Luther King III, is born

1958 September 17: Publishes *Stride Toward Freedom*

September 20: Stabbed during a book signing

1959 February: The Kings travel to India

November 29: Resigns position at the Dexter Avenue Baptist Church and accepts the position of co-pastor at the Ebenezer Baptist Church

1960 February 1: Student sit-ins begin in Greensboro, NC.

October 19: Arrested during a sit-in at Rich's Department Store

October 25: Sentenced to four months of hard labor at Reidsville State Penitentiary for violating parole

October 27: Senator John Kennedy intervenes

October 28: King is released on $2,000 bond

1961 January 3: Son Dexter is born.

May 4: Freedom Rides begin.

May 21: "Battle of Montgomery"

1962   July 10–12: King goes to jail in Albany, GA.
        September: Demonstrations begin in Birmingham
        October 1: James Meredith enrolls as first black
            student at University of Mississippi.
1963   March 28: Daughter, Bernice Albertine, is born
        April 3: Issues the "Birmingham Manifesto" and
            Project "C" begins
        April: Writes "Letter from a Birmingham Jail"
        August 28: Delivers "I have a dream . . ." address
            at the March on Washington
        December: Named *Time* magazine's "Man of the Year"
1964   June: Publishes *Why We Can't Wait*
        September: Kings visit West Berlin and Rome
        December 10: Receives the Nobel Peace Prize
1965   January 2: SCLC's first major rally in Selma is held
        March 21: Leads march from Selma to Montgomery
        Fall: Moves to Chicago to help the northern cause
1966   January: Forms the Chicago Freedom Movement
        June: The Meredith March reaches Jackson and over
            12,000 people gather to hear King's address
1967   April 4: Addresses audience on Vietnam at New
            York City's Riverside Church
        June: Publishes *Where Do We Go From Here? Chaos
            or Community*
        July: "Poor People's Campaign" is announced and
            "Operation Breadbasket" is expanded
1968   March 18: Addresses rally in Memphis and promises
            to lead march to support sanitation workers.
        April 4 : Assassinated by a gunman while
            standing on the balcony of the Lorraine Motel,
            Memphis

BIBLIOGRAPHY

BOOKS

Abernathy, Ralph David. *And the Walls Came Tumbling Down: An Autobiography*. New York: Harper and Row, 1989.

Albert, Peter J., and Ronald Hoffman, eds. *We Shall Overcome: Martin Luther King, Jr. and the Black Freedom Struggle*. New York: Pantheon Books, 1990.

Anderson, Jervis. *Bayard Rustin: Troubles I've Seen, A Biography*. New York: HarperCollins, 1997.

Anshoro, John J. *Martin Luther King, Jr.: The Making of a Mind*. Maryknoll, New York: Orbis Books, 1982.

Baldwin, James. *The Price of the Ticket*. New York: St. Martin's, 1985.

Bennett, Lerone, Jr. *What Manner of Man: A Biography of Martin Luther King, Jr.* Chicago: Johnson Publishing Co., 1964.

Branch, Taylor. *Parting the Waters: America in the King Years, 1954-1963*. New York: Simon and Schuster, 1988.

Brauer, Carl M. *John F. Kennedy and the Second Reconstruction*. New York: Columbia University Press, 1977.

Brisbane, Robert. *Black Activism: Racial Revolution in the United States, 1934-1970*. Valley Forge, PA: Judson Press, 1971.

Burk, Robert F. *The Eisenhower Administration and Black Civil Rights*. Knoxville: University of Tennessee Press, 1984.

Carson, Clayborne. *A Guide to Research on Martin Luther King, Jr., and the Modern Black Freedom Struggle*. Stanford, CA: Stanford University Libraries, 1989.

———— *In Struggle*: *SNCC and the Black Awakening of the 1960s*.
Cambridge, MA: Harvard University Press, 1981.

Carson, Clayborne, et al., eds. *The Papers of Martin Luther King*.
Vol. 1: Called to Serve. Berkeley: U. of California Press, 1992.

———— *The Papers of Martin Luther King Jr., Vol. 2: Rediscovering
Precious Values, July 1951–November 1955*. Berkeley:
U. of California Press, 1994.

———— *The Papers of Martin Luther King Jr., Vol. 3: Birth of a New
Age, December 1956*. Berkeley: U. of California Press, 1997.

Colaiaco, James H. *Martin Luther King, Jr.: Apostle of Militant
Nonviolence*. New York: St. Martin's Press, 1993.

Cone, James H. *Martin and Malcolm and America: A Dream or A
Nightmare*. Maryknoll, NY: Orbis Books, 1991.

Fairclough, Adam. *"To Redeem the Soul of America": The Southern
Christian Leadership Conference and Martin Luther King, Jr.*
Athens: University of Georgia Press, 1987.

Farmer, James. *Lay Bare the Heart: An Autobiography of the Civil
Rights Movement*. New York: Arbor House, 1986.

Franklin, V. P. *Black Self-Determination: A Cultural History of
African-American Resistance*. New York: Lawrence Hill, 1992.

———— *Living Our Stories, Telling Our Truths: Autobiography and the
Making of the African-American Intellectual Tradition*. New
York: Oxford University Press, 1996.

Garrow, David J. *Protest at Selma: Martin Luther King, Jr., and the
Voting Rights Act of 1965*. New Haven, CT: Yale U. Press, 1978.

———— *Bearing the Cross: Martin Luther King, Jr., and the Southern
Christian Leadership Conference*. New York: William Morrow, 1986.

———— *The Montgomery Bus Boycott and the Women Who Started It*.
Knoxville: University of Tennessee Press, 1987.

Graham, Hugh Davis. *The Civil Rights Era: Origins and Development
of National Policy, 1960–1965*. New York: Oxford U. Press, 1990.

Hamilton, Charles. *Adam Clayton Powell, Jr.: The Political*

Biography of an American Dilemma. New York: Collier, 1991.

Kapur, Sudarshan. *Raising Up a Prophet: The African-American Encounter with Gandhi.* Boston: Beacon Press, 1992.

King, Coretta Scott. *My Life with Martin Luther King, Jr.,* New York: Holt, Rinehart, Winston, 1969.

King, Martin Luther, Jr. *Stride Toward Freedom: The Montgomery Story.* New York: Harper, 1958.

———— *Why We Can't Wait.* New York: Harper and Row, 1964.

———— *Where Do We Go From Here? Chaos or Community.* Boston: Beacon Press, 1968.

King, Martin Luther, Sr., and Clayton Riley. *Daddy King: An Autobiography.* New York: William Morrow, 1980.

McAdam, Doug. *Freedom Summer.* New York: Oxford U. Press, 1988.

Malcolm X, and Alex Haley. *The Autobiography of Malcolm X.* New York: Grove Press, 1965.

Miller, Keith D. *Voice of Deliverance: The Language of Martin Luther King, Jr. and Its Sources.* New York: The Free Press, 1992.

Morris, Aldon D. *The Origins of the Civil Rights Movement: Black Communities Organizing for Change.* New York: Free Press, 1984.

Oates, Stephen B. *Let the Trumpet Sound.* New York: Harper, 1982.

O'Reilly, Kenneth. *"Racial Matters": The FBI's Secret File on Black America, 1960–1972.* New York: The Free Press, 1989.

Parks, Rosa, and Jim Haskins. *My Story.* New York: Dial, 1992.

Reddick, Lawrence D. *Crusader Without Violence: The Biography of Martin Luther King, Jr.,* New York: Harper, 1959.

Schlesinger, Arthur M. Jr. *Robert Kennedy and His Times.* New York: Ballantine, 1978.

Washington, James M. *A Testament of Hope: The Essential Writings of Martin Luther King, Jr.* New York: Harper and Row, 1986.

Williams, Juan. *Eyes on the Prize.* New York: Viking Press, 1987.

Young, Andrew. *An Easy Burden: The Civil Rights Movement and the Transformation of America.* New York: HarperCollins, 1996.

SOURCES

CHAPTER ONE

REFERENCES

Bennett; Carson: *Volume I*; King, Sr.; King Jr.: *Stride*; Oates.

SOURCES

p. 4 *"That call didn't come"*: King, Sr., p. 28.

p. 6 *"hundreds of people"*: Carson: *Volume I*, pp. 4–18.

p. 8 *"I took the necessary legal"*: King, Sr., p. 88.

p. 10 *"religious ideas and ideals"*: Carson: *Volume I*, p. 30.

p. 10 *"I Want to Be More"*: Oates, pp. 9–10.

p. 10 *Martin Luther King, Jr., was*: King, Sr., p. 126.

p. 11 *"I ain't gonna plow"*: ibid, p. 100.

p. 11 *"The climax came when"*: Carson: *Volume I*, p. 359.

p. 11 *"my mother took me on"*: King, Jr.: *Stride*, p. 19.

p. 11 *"I did not conquer"*: Carson: *Volume I*, p. 363.

p. 12 *"It was a night I'll"*: Bennett, p. 25.

p. 13 *"It was hard to understand"*: Carson: *Volume I*, p. 117.

p. 14 *"set forth a noble"* and ensuing: ibid, p. 363.

p. 15 *"Carried far enough"*: ibid, p. 236.

p. 15 *"a half-dozen books"*: Bennett, p. 37.

p. 17 *"actual and immediate"*: quoted in Carson, p. 413.

p. 17 *"there have been times"*: Carson: *Volume I*, p. 416.

CHAPTER TWO

REFERENCES

Abernathy; Carson: *Volume II*; King, Coretta; King, Sr.; Oates.

SOURCES

p. 20 *"really a nice girl"*: Oates, p. 42.

p. 22 *"Really no one"* and ensuing: King, Coretta, pp. 38–39.

p. 23 *"I will not go to Xenia"*: ibid, p. 43.

p. 23 *"I began to think"*: ibid, p. 52.

p. 23 *"You know, you"* and ensuing: ibid, pp. 55–56.

p. 24 *"I will be pastor"* and ensuing: ibid, p. 60–61.

p. 24 *"that it was"* and ensuing: King, Sr., pp. 150–51.

p. 25 *"we spent our"*: King, Coretta. p. 62

p. 26 *"to speak of God"* and ensuing: Carson: *Volume II*, p. 24–26.

p. 27 *"The length and the"* and ensuing: King, Coretta, pp. 7–8.

p. 29 *"it was an inevitable"*: ibid, pp. 96–97.

p. 31 *"I sat there burning with"* and ensuing: Abernathy, pp. 89–91.

CHAPTER THREE

REFERENCES

Abernathy; Carson: *In Struggle*; Fairclough; King, Coretta; King, Jr.: *Stride*; Morris; Oates; Parks; Washington

SOURCES

p. 35 *"People always say"* and ensuing: Parks, p. 116.

p. 36 *"I got registered in 1945"*: ibid, p. 76.

p. 38 *"It appears that the* Advertiser"*: ibid, p. 49.

p. 38 *"Martin, Martin,"*: King, Coretta, p. 115.

p. 39 *"Everyone paused, thought"*: Parks, pp. 133–34.

p. 39 *"Well, if you think"*: Abernathy, p. 148.

p. 40 *"had accepted favors"*: Parks, pp. 136–37.

p. 40 *"We will be"* and ensuing: King, Jr.: *Stride*, pp. 61–62.

p. 43 *"There would be no"* and ensuing: Parks, p. 147.

p. 44 *"there was a thunderous"* and ensuing: Abernathy, p. 162.

p. 45 *The concrete porch* and ensuing: King, Coretta, p. 127.

p. 45 *"to meet violence"*: King, Jr.: *Stride*, pp. 136–37.

p. 46 *"it turned out that"*: Abernathy, p. 168.

p. 46 *"an almost holiday"* and ensuing: King, Jr.: *Stride*, p. 146.

p. 48 *"The United States Supreme Court"*: ibid, p. 160.

p. 50 *"Lord, I hope no one"*: King, Jr.: *Stride,* p. 175.

p. 52 *"to redeem the soul of"*: Fairclough, p. 32.

p. 53 *"Give us the ballot"*: Washington, p. 198.

p. 53 *"we met with strong"*: Morris, p. 121.

p. 54 *"the SCLC had not"*: ibid, p. 115.

p. 56 *"If you don't"*: Oates, p. 134.

p. 56 *"The time has come"*: ibid, p. 136.

p. 58 *"Are you Dr. King"* and ensuing: King, Coretta, p. 169.

p. 59 *"History has thrust"*: Oates, p. 146.

p. 62 *"I feel that someone must"* and ensuing: ibid, pp. 159–60.

p. 63 *"stay in jail"*: King, Coretta, p. 174.

CHAPTER FOUR

REFERENCES

Carson: *In Struggle*; Garrow: *Bearing the Cross*; King, Coretta; King, Sr.; King, Jr.: *Why We Can't Wait*; Oates; Schlesinger; Williams; Young.

SOURCES

p. 66 *"shall not violate"*: Garrow: *Bearing the Cross*, p. 143.

p. 67 *"I think we must"* and ensuing: King, Coretta, p. 194–196.

p. 69 *"deeply indebted to Senator"* and ensuing: King, Sr., p. 176.

p. 69 *"No comment Nixon"*: Garrow: *Bearing the Cross*, p. 149.

p. 75 *"We can't tolerate"*: Carson: *In Struggle*, p. 60.

p. 76 *"before the victory"* and ensuing: Oates, p. 190–192.

p. 77 *"Growing up in"* and ensuing: Williams.

p. 79 *"we discovered"* and ensuing: Young, p. 171.

p. 79 *"unidentified Negro"* and ensuing: Carson: *In Struggle*, p. 61.

p. 80 *"Good, tell him to"*: Oates, p. 198.

p. 83 *"we decided on"* and ensuing: Garrow: *Bearing*, p. 228.

p. 85 *"just a dignified"*: Oates, p. 216.

p. 85 *"I spoke to 125 business"*: King: *Why We Can't Wait*, p. 54.

p. 86 *"I sat in the deepest"* and ensuing: ibid, p. 63.

p. 88 *"I have watched"*: Washington, pp. 3–6.

p. 89 *"I hope to subpoena"*: Oates, p. 233.

p. 90 *"Dammit. Turn"* and ensuing: King: *Why We Can't Wait*, p. 101.

p. 91 *"You go to a point"*: Oates, p. 240.

p. 91 *"satisfied his principles"* and ensuing: Young, p. 247.

p. 92 *"It is as old as"* and ensuing: Schlesinger, p. 369–370.

p. 93 *"in imitation of Gandhi's"* and ensuing: Young, p. 269.

CHAPTER FIVE
REFERENCES

Anderson; Baldwin; Garrow: *Bearing the Cross*; Hamilton; Oates; Schlesinger; Washington; Malcolm X; Young.

SOURCES

p. 95 *"massive Emancipation"* and ensuing: Anderson, p. 239.

p. 96 *There was no truth*: Hamilton, pp. 336–37.

p. 96 *"on the basis of"*: Baldwin, p. 261.

p. 98 *"You've got to get"* and ensuing: ibid, pp. 384–85.

p. 99 *"I started out reading"*: Garrow: *Bearing*, p. 283.

p. 100 *"I have a dream"*: ibid, p. 217.

p. 101 *"The innocent blood"*: Washington, pp. 221–22.

p. 102 *"frustration and despair"* and ensuing: ibid, p. 297.

p. 103 *"as the most dangerous"*: Oates, pp. 264–65.

p. 103 *"Bobby Kennedy resisted"*: Schlesinger, p. 387.

p. 103 *"I don't think"* and ensuing: Oates, p. 270–280.

p. 105 *"when a race riot occurs"*: Baldwin, p. 192.

p. 107 *"full and equal"*and ensuing: Civil Rights Act of 1964.

p. 112 *"the most notorious"* and ensuing: Garrow: *Bearing*, p. 360.

p. 113 *"determined to get"* and ensuing: Oates, p. 314.

p. 113 *"He was attempting to sell"* and ensuing: Young, pp. 318–19.

p. 114 *"a profound recognition"* and ensuing: Washington, pp. 225–26.

p. 114 *"I really wish I could just stay"*: Oates, p. 322.

CHAPTER SIX
REFERENCES

Fairclough; Garrow: *Bearing the Cross*; King, Jr.: *Where Do We Go*; Malcom X and Haley; Oates; Washington.

SOURCES

p. 119 *"determined, organized, mobilized"*: Fairclough, p. 229.

p. 119 *"a complete fraud"* and ensuing: Garrow: *Bearing*, p. 373.

p. 123 *"chickens coming home"*: Reported in many sources.

p. 123 *"conversion experience"* and ensuing: Malcom X and Haley.

p. 124 *"One has to conquer the fear"*: Garrow: *Bearing*, p. 393.

p. 124 *"the timidity of a federal government"* Fairclough, p. 241.

p. 127 *"classic example of trickery"*: Garrow: *Bearing*, p. 405.

p. 129 *"We are still in for"*: Washington, pp. 227–30.

p. 131 *"Some of the same things"* and ensuing: Oates, p. 367.

p. 131 *"The doctors tell me"* and ensuing: Garrow: *Bearing*, pp. 434–435.

p. 133 *"We won!"* and ensuing: King, Jr.: *Where Do We Go*, p. 112.

p. 134 *"I held back until it got"*: Garrow: *Bearing*, p. 430.

p. 135 *"and if something isn't done"*: Oates, p. 389.

CHAPTER SEVEN

REFERENCES

Carson: *In Struggle*; Fairclough; King, Jr.: *Where Do We Go*; Oates; Washington; Young.

SOURCES

p. 139 *"that desolate spot"*: King, Jr.: *Where Do We Go*, p. 25.

p. 141 *"black consciousness"* and ensuing: Fairclough, p. 313.

p. 143 *"This is the twenty-seventh time"* and ensuing: ibid, p. 316.

p. 148 *"I had expected"*: Garrow: *Bearing the Cross*, p. 500.

p. 151 *"far-reaching and creative"*: Fairclough, p. 302.

p. 151 *"to criticize details . . . in open"* and ensuing: CRR pp. 305–306.

p. 152 *"without placing"*: ibid, p. 360.

p. 158 *"when federal"* and ensuing: King: *Where Do We Go*, pp. 130–33.

p. 159 *"We're in terrible shape"*: Oates, pp. 457–58.

p. 159 *"If any of you are around"* and ensuing: Washington, p. 267.

p. 160 *"We are tired of being"* and ensuing: Oates, pp. 470–71.

p. 164 *"our sick white"* and ensuing: Washington, p. 286.

p. 164 *"we were all awed and shaken"*: Young, p. 463.

p. 168 *"to redeem the soul of America"*: Fairclough, p. 32.

PHOTOGRAPHY CREDITS

p. iv courtesy of UPI/Corbis-Bettmann

pp. 1, 34 courtesy of AP/Wide World Photos

p. 2 courtesy of UPI/Corbis-Bettmann

pp. 3, 13 courtesy of AP/Wide World Photos

p. 9 courtesy of AP/Wide World Photos

p. 18 courtesy of AP/Wide World Photos

pp. 19, 32 courtesy of Archive Photos

p. 21 courtesy of UPI/Corbis-Bettmann

pp. 35, 52 courtesy of AP/Wide World Photos

p. 37 courtesy of UPI/Corbis-Bettmann

p. 48 courtesy of AP/Wide World Photos

p. 54 courtesy of AP/Wide World Photos

p. 61 courtesy of AP/Wide World Photos

p. 64 © Henri Cartier-Bresson/Magnum Photos, Inc.

pp. 65, 66 courtesy of AP/Wide World Photos

p. 68 courtesy of AP/Wide World Photos

p. 75 courtesy of UPI/Corbis-Bettmann

p. 83 © Bruce Davidson/Magnum Photos, Inc.

p. 94 courtesy of AP/Wide World Photos

pp. 95, 102 courtesy of AP/Wide World Photos

p. 97 courtesy of AP/Wide World Photos

p. 100 courtesy of Archive Photos

p. 109 courtesy of UPI/Corbis-Bettmann

p. 116 courtesy of AP/Wide World Photos

pp. 117, 137 courtesy of AP/Wide World Photos

p. 120 courtesy of Archive Photos

p. 129 © Bruce Davidson/Magnum Photos, Inc.

p. 138 courtesy of AP/Wide World Photos

pp. 139, 143 courtesy of Express Newspapers/D-681/Archive Photos

p. 149 courtesy of AP/Wide World Photos

p. 165 courtesy of AP/Wide World Photos

p. 167 courtesy of AP/Wide World Photos

INDEX

Abernathy, Ralph 30–31, 53,
   71, 113, 119, 145, 166
   in Albany 76, 78–80
   in Birmingham 86–88, 91
   in Memphis 161–163, 165
   Montgomery bus boycott
      37–41, 43–46, 50
   in Selma 121, 126–128
Albany Movement 74–81
Baldwin, James 96, 105
Belafonte, Harry 84, 87, 167
Bevel, James 89, 93, 119, 122,
   134–135, 147–148, 150
Black Power 143–145, 154
Boston, MA 131
Brown v. Topeka Board of
   Education 29–30
Bunche, Ralph 55, 128
Bus boycott 36–51
Busing of students 131
Carmichael, Stokely 137,
   140–145
Civil Rights Act (1957) 53, 57,
   104

Civil Rights Act (1964) 92–93,
   98, 100, 103–104, 106–108
Civil Rights Act (1968) 168
Civil Rights Commission, U.S.
   53, 57, 107
Commerce Department 107
Communism 49, 84, 98, 103
Congress of Racial Equality
   (CORE) 70–71, 73, 137, 141
Connor, Bull 81–82, 85–87,
   89–92
Daley, Richard J. 136,
   146–148, 150–151
Democratic Party 57, 70, 110,
   112, 140–141, 155
Dexter Avenue Baptist Church,
   Montgomery 27–29, 59
DuBois, W. E. B. 99
Ebenezer Baptist Church,
   Atlanta 4–6, 14, 19, 25, 59
Eisenhower, Dwight D. 56, 57,
   67
Employment discrimination
   107

Evers, Medgar 93

Farmer, James 70–71, 73, 97, 113

Federal Bureau of Investigation (FBI) 84, 98, 102–103, 112–113, 119–120, 130, 159

Forman, James 73, 108, 127–128

Freedom Rides 70–73

Freedom Summer 108–110

Greensboro, NC 60

Hamer, Fannie Lou 110

Henry, Aaron 110

Hoover, J. Edgar 84, 102–103, 112–114, 119

Housing discrimination 147–152, 155–156, 168

Humphrey, Hubert 57, 168

India 58–59

Interstate transportation 70, 73–74, 78

Jackson, Jesse 135, 148–150, 156–157, 162, 165

Jackson, MS 72–73, 93, 145

Johns, Vernon 27, 28

Johnson, Lyndon B. 57, 62, 97, 104, 110, 112, 114–115, 121, 126–128, 132–134, 145, 154–155, 162–163, 166

Justice Department 53, 57, 84, 89

Katzenbach, Nicholas 121, 124–125

Kennedy, John F. 62–63, 69–70, 80, 87, 89, 92–93, 96–98, 100, 203

Kennedy, Robert F. 69, 71–73, 87, 91–93, 96–98, 103, 168

King, A. D. 10, 24, 69, 91–92, 164–165

King, Coretta Scott 20–24, 29, 44–45, 67–69, 119, 166, 168

King, Martin Luther, Sr. 3–4, 6, 10–11, 14, 20, 24–25, 46, 63, 69

King, Martin Luther, Jr.
arrests, trials, and sentences 43–44, 47, 56, 62–63, 65–68, 78–80, 87–88, 91
assassination and funeral 166–168
birth 6
books 56, 58, 108, 111, 139, 155, 158
boyhood and youth 8–12
children 32, 55, 80, 84
courtship and marriage 23–25
education, higher 12–17, 19–20, 25–27, 32
essays and manifestos 15, 85, 87–88, 101, 121
family background 3–6

newspaper and magazine columns 78

ordination 14

personality 104

prizes and awards 17, 53, 111–112, 114

race problem, early encounters with 11–13, 16

sermons and speeches 12, 27, 100, 154–155, 160, 164, 168

threats and violence against 44–45, 51, 58, 124–125, 159, 164

Ku Klux Klan 49, 105–106

Lawson, James 160–161, 165

Levison, Stanley 49, 51, 84, 98, 103, 154

Lewis, John 97, 108, 119–120, 125, 141

Liuzzo, Viola Gregg 130

Lowery, Joseph 53

Lowndes County, AL 140

McKissick, Floyd 137, 141–142, 144–145

Malcolm X 101–102, 123, 124

March on Washington 95–96, 98–102

Marshall, Burke 89–90

Marshall, Thurgood 53, 167

Meredith, James 136–137, 139

Mississippi 108–110, 136–137, 140, 142–146

Mississippi Freedom Democratic Party (MFDP) 110

Montgomery, AL 27–33, 36–51, 71–72, 129–130

National Association for the Advancement of Colored People (NAACP) 30–33, 35–36, 53–54, 74, 131, 142

New York City riots 110

Nixon, E. D. 33, 36–37, 46, 50

Nixon, Richard M. 67, 168

Nobel Prize 111–112, 114

Nonviolence 15, 45–46, 49, 51–52, 56, 80, 87–88, 114, 152

abandonment of 128, 133, 139, 141–145, 161–162

O'Dell, Jack 84, 98

Pacifism 15, 49

Parks, Rosa 33, 35–40, 43, 50

Personalism 14–15, 17, 20, 26

Poor People's Campaign 156–159

Powell, Adam Clayton 55–56, 96, 132

Raby, Al 148, 150–151

Randolph, A. Philip 52, 55–56, 95–98

Ray, James Earl 166

Rustin, Bayard 49, 51–52, 67, 96, 98, 112, 154

School desegregation 29–30, 33, 53–54, 57, 62, 107

Shuttlesworth, Fred 51, 71, 81–82, 88, 91

Sit-ins 60, 63, 85

Social gospel 6–7, 14

Southern Christian Leadership Conference (SCLC) 52–54, 59–60, 62, 73, 78, 96, 98, 111–112
  in Birmingham 81–83, 85–89
  in Chicago 134–136, 147–148
  in Louisville 155–156
  in Memphis 163
  in Mississippi 140, 142, 146
  Poor People's Campaign 156–158
  in Selma 118–122, 124–127
  in St. Augustine 106, 108

Store and restaurant desegregation 62–63, 65, 82, 85–86, 90–91

Student Nonviolent Coordinating Committee (SNCC) 61–62, 65, 70–71, 73–78, 108, 117–120, 124–128, 137, 139–143

Supreme Court, U.S. 29–30, 48–49

Vietnam War 124, 133–134, 145, 152–155, 162–163

Violence 44–45, 50–51, 72, 110, 137, 166
  in Birmingham 81–82, 92, 101
  in Chicago 146–147
  in Memphis 161–162
  in St. Augustine 106
  in Watts 133

Vivian, C. T. 105, 118, 122

Voting rights 53–55, 57, 59, 73–74, 78, 107–108, 111–112, 114–115, 117–119, 121–122, 128, 130, 140
  early campaigns for 10–11, 35–36

Voting Rights Act (1965) 132–133

Walker, Wyatt T. 70–71, 83, 88

Wallace, George 90, 92, 122, 125, 128

Washington, DC 132, 166

"We Shall Overcome" 77

White Citizens Council (WCC) 30

Wilkins, Roy 52–53, 56, 97–99, 141–142, 154

Williams, Hosea 105, 125, 130

Young, Andrew 79, 86, 91, 93, 106, 113–114, 119, 121, 164–166

Young, Whitney 97, 99, 141–142, 154

ACKNOWLEDGMENTS

In my earlier works on African-American cultural and intellectual history, I had not been able to devote sufficient time to an examination of the significant contributions of Dr. Martin Luther King, Jr., to twentieth-century U.S. and African-American history. I am happy that the editors at Balliett and Fitzgerald were able to afford me that opportunity. I am particularly grateful to Tom Dyja, Charlotte Sheedy, and Neeti Madan for their assistance in this project. Betty Collier-Thomas, Ed Collins, Mary Frances Berry, Melinda Chateauvert, Julie Mostov, Eric D. Brose, Sandra Bowen, Antonio Barrales Dafos, Aubrey McCoy, and Edward McDonald provided me with the intellectual sustenance for this welcome endeavor.

The bulk of the writing for the book was completed while I was serving as a Fulbright professor at the Universidad de Barcelona and the Universidad Autónoma de Barcelona in Spain. I was happy I was able to use Dr. King's life and activities as a lens through which to view twentieth-century U.S. history. I want to thank my students, especially Teresa Requena, Isabel Quintana Wulf, Ramon Andreu i Ahmed, Astrid Lozano Villó, Juan Carlos Batalla Callau, Maria Eulalia Carceller Guillamet, Marta Cantamisa Mercadal, Sandra Martínez Salvans, Mónica Pons Soldado, Ana Maria Mena Sóñora, Ana María Fuente Rullo, Montse Roig Viladoms, Mercé Diago Esteva, Eva Codó Olsina, Manel Molina Muños, and Judith Garrido Baldé. I also benefited from my conversations with my colleagues at the Universidad de Barcelona, especially Angels Carabi, Rodigo Andres, and Enric

Montforte. The Fulbright officials, María Jesús Pablos and Patricia Zahniser, provided me with the support I needed to enjoy my stay in Spain and to complete this project.

ABOUT THE AUTHOR

V. P. Franklin is professor of history at Drexel University. He received his Ph.D. from the University of Chicago, and has taught United States and African-American history at Yale University, Arizona State, and the University of Illinois, and as a Fulbright professor at the Universidad de Barcelona and the Universidad Autónoma de Barcelona in Spain. Dr. Franklin is the co-editor of *New Perspectives on Black Educational History* (1978), and the author of *The Education of Black Philadelphia* (1979), *Black Self-Determination: A Cultural History of African-American Resistance* (1992), and numerous essays on African-American history and education. His most recent book is *Living Our Stories, Telling Our Truths: Autobiography and the Making of the African-American Intellectual Tradition* (1996).